D1068188

Critical Issues in Asset Building in Singapore's Development

Happy Reading

Other Related Titles from World Scientific

50 Years of Social Issues in Singapore
edited by David Chan
foreword by Tharman Shanmugaratnam
ISBN: 978-981-4696-91-3 (box-set)
ISBN: 978-981-4632-60-7
ISBN: 978-981-4632-61-4 (pbk)

Liveability in Singapore: Social and Behavioural Issues
edited by David Chan
ISBN: 978-981-4667-87-6

Social Futures of Singapore Society
edited by David Chan
ISBN: 978-981-3222-22-9

50 Years of Urban Planning in Singapore
edited by Chye Kiang Heng
ISBN: 978-981-4656-45-0
ISBN: 978-981-4656-46-7 (pbk)

Critical Issues in Asset Building in Singapore's Development

Editors

S Vasoo
National University of Singapore, Singapore

Bilveer Singh
National University of Singapore, Singapore

 **World Scientific**

NEW JERSEY · LONDON · SINGAPORE · BEIJING · SHANGHAI · HONG KONG · TAIPEI · CHENNAI · TOKYO

Published by

World Scientific Publishing Co. Pte. Ltd.

5 Toh Tuck Link, Singapore 596224

USA office: 27 Warren Street, Suite 401-402, Hackensack, NJ 07601

UK office: 57 Shelton Street, Covent Garden, London WC2H 9HE

Library of Congress Cataloging-in-Publication Data
Names: Vasoo, S., editor. | Singh, Bilveer, 1956– editor. |
    Sherraden, Michael W. (Michael Wayne), 1948– Challenges in asset building in Singapore.
Title: Critical issues in asset building in Singapore's development / [edited by]
    S. Vasoo, Bilveer Singh.
Description: New Jersey : World Scientific, [2018] | Includes bibliographical references and index.
Identifiers: LCCN 2018016255 | ISBN 9789813239753 (hardcover)
Subjects: LCSH: Singapore--Social policy. | Human capital--Singapore. |
    Human services--Singapore. | Public administration--Singapore.
Classification: LCC HN700.67.A8 C75 2018 | DDC 306.095957--dc23
LC record available at https://lccn.loc.gov/2018016255

British Library Cataloguing-in-Publication Data
A catalogue record for this book is available from the British Library.

For any available supplementary material, please visit
http://www.worldscientific.com/worldscibooks/10.1142/10976#t=suppl

Desk Editor: Jiang Yulin

Typeset by Stallion Press
Email: enquiries@stallionpress.com

Printed in Singapore

About the Contributors

Hongbo Jia has a PhD in Economics. Currently he is an Associate Professor and the Deputy Director of the Social Security Institute of Beihang University. His primary area of expertise is public administration, and his research focuses on the reform of pension, medical insurance and health care system in China. As a Visiting Scholar, he worked at the National University of Singapore (NUS) in 2010 and at the Australian National University (ANU) from 2014 to 2015.

Ching Leong is Assistant Professor and the Co-Director of the Institute of Water Policy at the Lee Kuan Yew School of Public Policy, National University of Singapore (NUS). Leong's work lies in making sense of apparently irrational environmental behaviour, whether poor decision-making relating to water use in households, risk taking in drinking recycled water, investing in water utilities, to building dams and managing rivers. She uses narratives, perceptions and stories to understand collective public behaviour, and how these provide elements of environmental identities. Her research is premised on the idea that an environmental identity emotionally and cognitively connects an individual's perceptions, beliefs, values and habits with elements of the natural environment. Leong has a PhD in Public Policy from NUS and graduate degrees in philosophy, information technology and journalism. She had previously worked as a newspaper and television reporter.

Bernard F.W. Loo is Associate Professor and Coordinator of the Master of Science (Strategic Studies) degree programme at the S. Rajaratnam School of International Studies (RSIS), Nanyang Technological University. He completed his doctoral studies at the Department of International Politics at the University of Wales, Aberystwyth in 2002. He is the author of *Medium Powers and Accidental Wars: A Study in Conventional Strategic Stability* (Edwin Mellen, 2005). His edited volume, *Military Transformation and Operations* (Routledge, 2009), was translated into complex Chinese for the Taiwanese military. His other publications have appeared in the *Journal of Strategic Studies*, *Contemporary Southeast Asia*, *NIDS Security Reports*, and *Taiwan Defense Affairs*. He is a regular commentator on defence matters, and his commentaries have appeared in *The Straits Times* (Singapore), *The Nation* (Thailand), and *The New Straits Times* (Malaysia). He has been invited to speak at a variety of defence-related institutions and conferences in China, Estonia, Finland, Japan, New Zealand, Norway, the Philippines and Taiwan. His research interests encompass defence policy, war studies, strategic theory, conventional military strategies, strategic challenges of small and medium powers, and problems and prospects of military transformation.

Irene Y.H. Ng is Associate Professor at the Department of Social Work and Director, Social Service Research Centre at the Faculty of Arts and Social Sciences, National University of Singapore. She holds a joint PhD in Social Work and Economics from the University of Michigan. Her research areas include poverty and inequality, intergenerational mobility, youth crime, and social welfare policy. Her research projects include an evaluation of a national Work Support programme; National Youth Surveys 2010, 2013 and 2017; a study of low-income households with debt; and an evaluation of Social Service Offices. She is active in the community, serving or having served in committees in the Ministry of Social and Family Development, National Council of Social Service, Ministry of Manpower, and various voluntary welfare organisations. Her teaching areas include poverty, policy, welfare economics, youth work, and programme planning.

Norshahril Saat, PhD is a Fellow at the Institute of Southeast Asian Studies (ISEAS)-Yusof Ishak Institute. In June 2015, he was awarded a PhD in International, Political and Strategic Studies by the Australian National University (ANU). He is a recipient of the Islamic Religious Council of Singapore (MUIS) Post-graduate Scholarship 2011. In 2015, he became the first recipient of Syed Isa Semait Scholarship (SISS), the highest honour for a MUIS scholar. His research interests are mainly on Southeast Asian politics and contemporary Islamic thought. In 2018, he published *The State, Ulama and Islam in Malaysia and Indonesia* (Amsterdam University Press), and his other earlier books include *Faith, Authority and the Malays: The Ulama in Contemporary Singapore; and Yusof Ishak: Singapore's First President.* His articles have recently been published in journals such as *Contemporary Islam: Dynamics of Muslim Life, Review of Indonesian and Malaysian Affairs, Studia Islamika*, and *Asian Journal of Social Science.* He has also published numerous opinion and think pieces, including those in local newspapers such as *The Straits Times, Berita Harian* and *Today,* and international newspapers such as the *The Canberra Times, Bangkok Post*, and *The Jakarta Post.*

Michael Sherraden is G.W. Brown Distinguished University Professor, Washington University in St. Louis and concurrently the S. R. Nathan Visiting Professor, National University of Singapore. He is the founding director of the Centre for Social Development (CSD) at the Brown School. Working with colleagues at CSD and many partners, Sherraden creates and tests innovations to improve social and economic well-being. He has defined and informed a growing body of applied research and policy to promote inclusion in asset building. This work has influenced asset-based policies and programmes in many countries. His research results have also informed inclusive and progressive child development accounts (CDAs) in many countries. In addition, Sherraden's research on Civilian Conservation Corps of the 1930s contributed to the creation of AmeriCorps, and he was in attendance for the signing of the bill at the White House. Sherraden was elected to the inaugural class of the American Academy of Social Work and Social Welfare, serves on the board, and is a co-director of the national initiative Grand Challenges for Social Work. Among other awards, he has been a Fulbright Scholar and listed by TIME magazine as one of the 100 most influential people in the world. Sherraden's teaching currently focuses on social policy, social innovation, and effective strategies in applied social science.

Bilveer Singh is Associate Professor at the Department of Political Science, National University of Singapore and an Adjunct Senior Fellow at the Centre of Excellence for National Security, S. Rajaratnam School of International Studies, Nanyang Technological University. He received his MA and PhD in International Relations from the Australian National University. His research covers Singapore's politics and foreign policy as well as security issues in the Southeast Asia region with a particular focus on terrorism.

S Vasoo is Associate Professorial Fellow at the Department of Social Work, National University of Singapore. He obtained his Doctorate and Master of Social Work from the University of Hong Kong and holds a Diploma in Social Studies with distinction from the University of Singapore. He authored a number of monographs on social issues and has published various articles both internationally and locally. He was awarded the Honorary Life Member of the Singapore Association of Social Workers for his outstanding contributions to social work in Singapore. He was the Member of Parliament from 1984 to 2001 and he also served as Chairman of Government Parliamentary Committee for Community Development. He is Advisor to a number of Voluntary Welfare Organisations in Singapore.

Yishu Zhou is a Research Associate at the Institute of Water Policy at the Lee Kuan Yew School of Public Policy, National University of Singapore. She has a Masters in Comparative Politics from the London School of Economics and a degree in Philosophy and Politics from the University of York.

Contents

List of Tables

List of Figures

Abbreviations

AMP	Association of Muslim Professionals
AP	Aggregate Percentage
ARPS	Approved Residential Properties Scheme
CC	Community Club/Centre
CC SMTA	ComCare Short-to-Medium Term Assistance
CDA	Child Development Account
CDAC	Chinese Development Assistance Council
CDC	Community Development Council
CMC	Community Mediation Centre
CMIO	Chinese, Malays, Indians and Others
CNA	*Channel NewsAsia*
CPF	Central Provident Fund
EP	Elected President
FDI	Foreign Direct Investment
FSC	Family Service Centre
FSHS	Fresh Start Housing Scheme
GDP	Gross Domestic Product
GRC	Group Representation Constituency
HDB	Housing and Development Board
HIP	Home Improvement Programme
HUDC	Housing and Urban Development Company
IDA	Individual Development Account
IDWA	Index of Drinking Water Adequacy

ILO	International Labour Organization
IPS	Institute of Policy Studies
IRHS	Interim Rental Housing Scheme
IRO	Inter-Religious Organisation
JI	*Jemaah Islamiyah*
KL	Kuala Lumpur
LBS	Lease Buyback Scheme
LE	Life Expectancy at Birth
LSA	Letter of Social Assessment
LUP	Lift Upgrading Programme
MCA	Malaysian Chinese Association
MCP	Malayan Communist Party
MHA	Ministry of Home Affairs
MIC	Malaysian Indian Congress
MOE	Ministry of Education
MOP	Minimum Occupation Period
MP	Member of Parliament
MRT	Mass Rapid Transit
MSF	Ministry of Social and Family Development
MUIS	Islamic Religious Council of Singapore
MUP	Main Upgrading Programme
NCMP	Non-Constituency Member of Parliament
NGO	Non-Governmental Organisation
NMP	Nominated Member of Parliament
NRP	Neighbourhood Renewal Programme
NS	National Service
NTILs	Non-Tamil Indian Languages
NTUC	National Trades Union Congress
OB	Out-of-Bounds Markers
PAP	People's Action Party
PCF	PAP Community Foundation
POSB	Post Office Savings Bank
PSEA	Post-Secondary Education Account
PUB	Public Utilities Board
RC	Residents' Committee
RRG	Religious Rehabilitation Group

RUAS	Rent and Utilities Assistance Scheme
SAF	Singapore Armed Forces
SG100	Singapore 100
SINDA	Singapore Indian Development Association
SMC	Single Member Constituency
SOC	Special Operations Command
TC	Town Council
TRS	*The Real Singapore*
UMNO	United Malays National Organisation
UN	United Nations
VWO	Voluntary Welfare Organisation
WP	Workers' Party
WSP	Work Support Programme

Acknowledgements

We wish to express our heartfelt thanks and appreciation to the many people who assisted us in one way or another in completing and bringing out this edited volume. First and foremost, we are grateful to the authors for coming on board the project on 'asset building in Singapore' and agreeing to publish their chapters as part of the edited volume. Our gratitude goes to Michael Sherraden, Norshahril Saat, Hongbo Jia, Irene Ng, Yishu Zhou, Ching Leong and Bernard Loo.

We are also indebted to World Scientific, especially Mr. Jiang Yulin, in bringing out this study, which was professionally undertaken with patience and great support.

It is our expectation that this publication will add to the existing literature on Singapore's development and more importantly, create greater awareness of how citizens' assets have been meticulously built and enhanced over the last 50 years or so.

In the final analysis, while the authors are responsible for their respective chapters, we take full responsibility for any error that may occur in the book.

S Vasoo
Bilveer Singh
June 2018

Introduction

S Vasoo and Bilveer Singh

Stable social and political conditions are primarily significant for any state to enhance the lives of its people and without these precursors, no social and economic progress could be achieved. More importantly, people-centric leadership is indeed critical to bring about improvements to people's livelihood. As can be seen in many places, self-centric leadership has brought about immense social and economic hardships to various communities. One can look around the world, and see that societies with self-serving leaders who lack honesty and integrity, have regressed down the social and economic ladder. When people suffer and experience no improvement to their well-being, they often migrate to seek better future for themselves and their families. Therefore, one can identify that some major critical issues in political and social development do contribute to the health of societies. In the case of Singapore, there are a number of key factors that have helped to facilitate the country's growth and development. These will be discussed in the various presentations in this volume.

It is noted that issues of race and religion have surfaced in a number of developed and developing countries where their communities have been fractured by racial and religious disharmony. Racial and religious strifes are now more common in a number of societies and once started, they spread like wild fires which cannot be doused easily.

The world is seeing many serious negative consequences as a result of the rise in religious and racial discourses and many societies face serious recurring loss of lives and properties. Fortunately, Singapore despite facing racial and religious riots in the early years after its independence, was able to confront this problem by implementing stringent and no-nonsense legislative policies to tackle groups propounding race and religious divisions. With merit-based social and public policies, education, social integration and equal opportunities for all, any heinous setbacks have been kept in abeyance so far.

More often than not, policy makers tend to give much attention to economic policies while playing down the social and political dimensions and issues. A good holistic thrust covering a sensible balance of socio-economic and political grounds will be essential for furthering Singapore's progress. One cannot overlook that social and human capitals are important in community building and more attention has to be paid to develop Singapore's population talent without which slower progress will come about as less talents will be around to drive the engine of Singapore's future progress.

Policy makers can assist by allocating more resources to improve more opportunities to help many low-income children who otherwise may be ill-equipped to benefit from education and skills training opportunities. In the longer term, the social divide may be further widened when more low-income children fail to acquire the knowledge and skills that can prepare them to earn a livelihood, not only in Singapore, but also globally. When the social gap widens, the consequences will not be good for the Singapore community, as a divided community may be socially unhealthy for Singapore. We can engage families in the low-income group to participate in early head-start programmes which can enable the children to be more numerate and literate. Family-matched saving projects to help low-income families become more financially literate and to better motivate them to upgrade their skills could be implemented.

The idea of savings was first initiated more than 50 years ago. The Post Office Savings Bank (POSB) started a saving scheme for students, where primary school students would purchase stamps and stick them on a pre-prepared card and once the card was completed, the amount of money would be credited into the student's account. Therein began the financial asset building for school students in Singapore and this approach has never really disappeared. Only that it has become more enhanced, sophisticated and widespread asset building in Singapore encompassing a whole array of elements that have helped to build an empowered society involving all levels of the economic strata. The baby bonuses of today and the various medical insurance schemes such as MediSave, MediShield Life, MediFund and ElderShield are part and parcel of this approach of helping Singapore citizens in the accumulation of assets.

With globalisation, it is envisaged that Singapore, like other developed economies, will be confronted with more competition from developing economies with both skilled and unskilled manpower for market share for product and services. This situation will be inevitable, and the likelihood is that wages will be depressed as the services offered by the developing world will be cheaper, more efficient and more effective. So, to meet these challenging scenarios, Singapore has little option but to take steps to train every young child and adult with higher skills in areas such as marine and biological sciences, medicine and pharmacy, chemical and nanotechnology, food safety and production, precision and aeronautical engineering, building and housing construction, and environmental and water resource technology.[1]

In the coming decade the world will become more globalised; therefore, Singaporeans must acquire more analytical skills in order to gather information that will predict more precisely emerging social problems. In doing so, more effective social solutions and problem-solving strategies can be implemented. More importantly, one must not use old approaches to tackle new emerging social problems. In short, it is critical to look for good innovative ways to solve social and political development issues.

---

[1] These points have been reflected in several papers by S Vasoo, for instance, in "Social work in response to challenging times", *Asia Pacific Journal of Social Work*, 23(4), pp. 315–318, 2013 and unpublished notes on "Social Challenges Facing Singapore", 2013.

In Singapore, building a populace's assets and instituting stabilisers in the political system are some of the keys to good governance. If anything, a well-endowed populace can be a source of political stability just as a population that is deprived and with unsettled liabilities, especially financial ones, can lead to immense political instability, through public unhappiness and grievances, especially if the public's financial insecurity is caused by government policies. Asset building is for all, the rich, middle class and the poor even though most research works have focused on asset accumulation for the lower-income groups.[2]

A major thinker and contributor to this approach of asset building and development is Professor Michael Sherraden, the Benjamin E. Youngdahl Professor of Social Development at the Brown School at Washington University in St. Louis, US.[3] According to Sherraden's landmark study released in 1991 titled *Assets and the Poor: A New American Welfare Policy*,[4] asset accumulation is structured and subsidised for the "non-poor households, primarily via retirement accounts and home ownership."[5] While this was helpful in enriching a largely already endowed segment of the population, he argued that similar opportunities should also be made available to all, especially the low-income groups. In this regard, Sherraden proposed the establishment of saving accounts for the poor individuals called Individual Development Accounts (IDAs).[6]

For Sherraden, the idea was to "offer a development account to everyone that begins at birth. Money could accumulate in these

[2] For example, see Signe-Mary McKernan and Michael Sherraden (eds.), *Asset building and low-income families* (Washington, D.C.: The Urban Institute Press, 2008).

[3] See Mark Schreiner, Michael Sherraden, Margaret Clancy, Lissa Johnson, Jami Curley and Min Zhan, *et al.*, "Assets and the poor: Evidence from Individual Development Accounts", in Michael Sherraden and Lisa Morris (eds.), *Inclusion in the American Dream: Assets, poverty and public policy* (Oxford, England: Oxford University Press, 2005).

[4] Michael Sherraden, *Assets for the poor: A new American welfare policy* (New York: M.E. Sharpe, 1991).

[5] See Jessica Martin, "Impact of assets and the poor grows 20 years after its release", *The Source*, 13 December 2011. Retrieved from https://source.wustl.edu/2011/12/impact-of-assets-and-the-poor-grows-20-years-after-its-release/

[6] Jessica Martin, "Impact of assets and the poor grows 20 years after its release".

accounts and matching would be progressive, with lower-income families receiving a higher contribution."[7] After more than 25 years of Sherraden's work and where many of his ideas have been adopted by governments in the United States, United Kingdom, China, Canada, South Korea and Singapore, there is "evidence that when there are savings and assets in the household — particularly savings in a child's name — children have greater educational attainment, are more likely to do well in high schools, attend college and graduate from college."[8] In short, asset building, especially for the poor, can have a positive impact in uplifting citizens' financial capacity.

To commence the discussion on assets, it is important to distinguish it from incomes. According to Sherraden, incomes are flows of resources and where people can receive incomes in return for their labour and use of capital. On the other hand, assets are stocks of resources which people have accumulated over time. Assets are important in helping people to tide over future contingencies and hence a source of security.[9] This has led to the acceptance as public policy that income and promotion of consumption alone are insufficient to ensure an individual's and community's well-being. Instead, an asset-based policy would be far more important and useful in ensuring growth and stability.

In common sense language, assets refer to an individual's wealth and possessions of value. In his 1991 work, Sherraden described assets as "tangibles" and "intangibles". This could include the following: money that is saved; stocks, bonds and different types of financial securities; property; assets such as jewellery, art pieces and automobiles; machines and other components of production; household goods; natural resources; and items of value such as patents, copyrights, etc.[10]

Others have adopted a broader definition of what can constitute as one's assets. Some view assets as simply anything of value that can

---

[7] Jessica Martin, "Impact of assets and the poor grows 20 years after its release".

[8] Jessica Martin, "Impact of assets and the poor grows 20 years after its release".

[9] See Signe-Mary McKernan and Michael Sherraden (eds.), *Asset building and low-income families*, p. viii.

[10] Michael Sherraden, *Assets and the poor: A new American welfare policy*.

be converted into cash. These could be liquid and illiquid assets. While liquid assets can be easily and quickly converted into cash (stocks, money market instruments and government bonds), illiquid assets are not that easily convertible to cash and these can include items such as houses, land and antiques.

In general, however, assets are best understood by categorising them into two types, namely tangible and intangible assets. An individual's or even a company's tangible assets could include cash at hand or in the bank, inventories and land. As for the intangible assets, these can encompass software, websites and even patented technologies.

In this regard, when discussing the issue of asset building, it basically involves how government policies are crafted to enhance an individual's tangible and intangible assets. It is about empowering one's citizen financially so that the citizen can feel that there is an upward mobility in terms of his resources and items of value.

If income and consumption alone are necessary but not sufficient conditions to ensure growth, equity and stability, for the purpose of this study, understanding what asset would encompass is equally important and necessary. There is a need for a holistic approach to ensure an individual's well-being, in turn, having a positive knock-on effect to guarantee a nation's peace and resilience. In this context, assets include not only measures in enhancing directly an individual's financial accounts but also a series of measures that will ensure societal growth, peace, development and eventually legitimacy of the political system that generates these policies. To that extent, in a broad sense, the introduction of a whole array of political, economic, social-cultural and even military-strategic policies can encompass a nation's process of asset building. In this regard, introduction of what has been described as political stabilisers in a political system can also be viewed as part and parcel of a nation's asset-building policies.

In Singapore, while asset building has been a long-standing policy, accompanying it is the policy of instituting stabilisers in the political system so that the individual's assets can be enhanced by living and operating in a political structure that guarantees the continued enhancement of one's assets. It is about building all-round stability that will safeguard and enhance one's acquired wealth and assets rather than lead to its depreciation.

In a parliamentary speech in January 2016, Prime Minister Lee Hsien Loong, in announcing wide-ranging changes to the political system, justified the changes on grounds that:

> *It is not possible for any political system to guarantee a country political stability and prosperity forever. But we can make such a happy outcome more likely if we design our system carefully and correctly around the core principles: Ensure high-quality government, keep our politics open and contestable, maintain accountability for the Government, uphold a multiracial society, and institute suitable stabilisers and checks and balances in the system.[11]*

Prime Minister Lee also stated that:

> *Nobody can predict the future or tell how our needs will change. If the system is to serve future generations well, then it is our responsibility to keep it up-to-date — regularly recalibrated, adjusted and improved, while preserving the principles that it was built upon.[12]*

Against this backdrop, it is clear that whether it is for developed or developing nations, asset building is increasingly seen as an important part of nation building and good governance. This is because appropriate social policies aimed at people's asset building can create the conditions and anchors for political, economic and social stability.

Singapore has often been cited as being unique in developing all-round social policies aimed at asset building of its citizens. This has helped to provide stability anchors at all levels of society, be it politically, economically and socially. Some have described Singapore's

---

[11] See Zakir Hussain, "Changes to political system to prepare Singapore for long term: PM Lee Hsien Loong", *The Straits Times*, 28 January 2016.
[12] Zakir Hussain, "Changes to political system to prepare Singapore for long term: PM Lee Hsien Loong".

approach as one of 'inclusive asset building'. The approach is not new as it has been implemented since the early 1960s and refined over the years.

Singapore's asset-building policies for its population can be most clearly seen from its manifold public policies such as the Central Provident Fund (CPF) and public housing scheme. Singapore has developed and adopted institutional saving policies that have served to benefit its citizens over the long run. In addition to CPF and public housing, the emphasis on the development of a corrupt-free polity, focus on skills development of its people, emphasis on social order and harmony, political accommodation and inclusive defence policies based on its citizenry are elements of this policy.

An asset-building approach to governance has been increasingly seen as being vital for political stability. As globalisation gradually widens the disparity between the 'haves' and 'have-nots' as well as increases the movement of labour and capital, there is an urgent need to provide stability for the populace, especially in times of crisis. What happens when a portion of the citizens loses their jobs for one reason or another? What happens when an employed citizen ages and no longer has the means to support himself, especially for medical care and other basic needs? These are critical questions that will confront any society, what more a small resource-less state such as Singapore.

To flesh out Singapore's broad-based, inclusive asset-building policy, a number of areas will be analysed for study and research. This will include discussion of social issues in Singapore, how housing is part of asset building, the policy on retirement benefits and health-care, developing national skills and talent, Singapore's approach to multiracialism and development of an inclusive political system, and how defence policy is part of the nation's asset-building policy.

This study is made up of eight chapters. Chapter 1, by Michael Sherraden, the doyen of studies on assets, examines the concept of asset building in general and its application to states as part of wealth creation and the uplifting of citizens' welfare. In Chapter 2, S Vasoo explores the various facets of social issues in Singapore. Norshahril Saat, in Chapter 3, analyses the issues involving multiracialism and multiculturalism. In Chapter 4, Bilveer Singh discusses the role of political innovations as stabilisers in Singapore. Hongbo Jia and S Vasoo in Chapter 5 analyses the role of housing as an important asset building for Singapore's citizens. In Chapter 6, Irene Y.H. Ng presents the challenges facing low-income families and measures undertaken to build their assets. In Chapter 7, Yishu Zhou and Ching Leong look at the management of water resources as part of asset building in Singapore. Finally, in Chapter 8, Bernard F.W. Loo analyses the role of national conscription Singapore's asset building.

Looking into the future, Singapore's asset-building capacity for socio-economic development will depend not only the changing socio-political landscape of the countries in the region and their willingness for mutual co-operation and partnership but also the ageing population in Singapore. With the danger of a decline in population, Singapore's productivity and ability to generate resources will be in question and the solution to this problem is to encourage population growth through increasing family size to three or more and by attraction of selective talents from overseas. Also, to enhance our talent pool, it is timely to review the educational streaming policy at an early age as this can have a labelling effect on the self-confidence and image of students who can become socially and psychologically affected. The consequences will be that the potential abilities of children who are slow developers but have hidden abilities at that point of their lives can be missed and streamed out inadvertently. With the complements of better compensatory educational support or early educational intervention programmes, quite a number of the talents can be helped to bloom later. Unless Singapore takes steps to think out of the box in finding positive ways to ensure its survival by renewal and rejuvenation of its socio-economic and environmental systems, this could result in a geriatric and status quo society with less drive and a heavy burden for the coming younger generation who will have an uphill climb to push further in maintaining Singapore's continued progress and vibrancy.

Chapter 1

Challenges in Asset Building in Singapore

Michael Sherraden

Introduction

Asset building as a social policy innovation is a relative "newcomer" in policy discussions and research. Asset building can be a very broad concept, referring to positive conditions in many aspects of an economy and society. In this chapter, the term asset building is used somewhat more specifically, referring to the policy goal of widespread accumulation of financial and tangible wealth in households to be used for social support and development. This definition may be useful in focusing attention on a particular policy system in Singapore, which is expressed in a portfolio of applications (policy schemes) and outcomes (social and economic changes). This definition also enables a clarification of the difference between income-based social policy (which is dominant in almost advanced nations) and asset-based policy (which is dominant in Singapore).

Singapore has led in asset-based policy since the 1960s, and is today the most advanced example of inclusive asset-building policy. Asset building has become the backbone of Singapore's strategy for social and economic development of households, with applications in housing, insurance protections, healthcare, education, and many

1

other areas. Asset-building policy is not primarily about money, but rather about family and society development.

While no policy is perfect, Singaporean policy has achieved a number of positive outcomes. It has generated perhaps the highest homeownership rate in the world, with most low-income households having a positive net worth, providing a degree of stability in the face of a global trend towards greater income inequality. This chapter places Singapore's asset-building policy in context, and somewhat in comparison with policies in the United States and most developed economies.

In practice, asset-based policy is a system of accounts where assets accumulate with the guidance and assistance of government design, regulation, and subsidy, to be used for a wide range of social purposes. Ideally, as a public policy, asset building would be fully inclusive — universal, progressive, and lifelong. Singapore has taken significant steps towards this ideal. The process of policy development in Singapore is active and continuous, adapting to social and economic challenges as they arise across time and circumstance.

A Half Century of Social Policy Innovation in Singapore[1]

Singapore's history

Singapore as a sovereign nation was expelled from the Malaysia Federation in 1965 — small and vulnerable, facing geopolitical and ethnic/religious hostilities, with no natural resources. Many residents of Singapore were migrants who did not identify with the new nation. Many were surviving on inadequate incomes and living in substandard housing. Survival of Singapore as a nation was not at all certain. This challenging beginning has significantly shaped Singapore's distinctive

---

[1] This section borrows from a Public Lecture at Singapore's 50th Anniversary as an Independent Nation, National University of Singapore, March 2015, and a Keynote Lecture at Conference of the International Consortium on Social Development, SIM University, Singapore, July 2015.

social and economic policies, leading step-by-step to impressive development over the next 50 plus years.[2]

Credit for growth is not due to economic strategy alone, but also — and perhaps foremost — to social innovations.[3] The state in Singapore is actively shaping social institutions and practices.[4] Purposeful emphasis on social development was articulated by national founding figures Lee Kuan Yew, Goh Keng Swee, and others. Mr. Lee and Dr. Goh had attended university in the United Kingdom and knew first-hand the post-war social welfare policies of "the welfare state." They did not believe the new Singapore state could afford these policies. Singaporean leadership took the practical position of doing what might work in a threatened and very small country with few resources. They focused first on education, housing, and healthcare. If these were provided, they reasoned, people could develop to reach their potential, be productive, and support their families.[5]

When the International Labour Organization (ILO) visited Singapore in the 1960s, urging leaders to set up a social insurance system for retirement, which had become standard in Western Europe, the new Prime Minister Lee and his chief economic advisor Goh listened and thanked the ILO officials, but did not accept their suggestion. Instead, they set about expanding the existing Central Provident Fund (CPF). Provident funds had been set up in the British colonies as an inferior retirement system — which some Singaporeans

---

[2] Shashi Jayakumar and Rahul Sagar (eds.), *The big ideas of Lee Kuan Yew* (Singapore: Straits Times Press, 2015).

[3] Shanmugaratnam, T., "Inclusive housing and social equity", keynote speech at international conference sponsored by Washington University and National University of Singapore (Next Age Institute), Duke University, and Brookings Institution (host), Washington, D.C., November 2015.

[4] Kalyani Mehta and Ann Wee, (eds.), *Social Work in the Singapore Context* (Singapore: Pearson Publishing, 2011); S.R. Nathan, *An Unexpected Journey: Path to the Presidency* (Singapore: Editions Didier Millet, 2011); and Jamet Salaff, *State and family in Singapore* (Ithaca, NY: Cornell University Press, 1990).

[5] Michael Sherraden, Interview with Goh Keng Swee, National University of Singapore, 1992; Michael Sherraden, Interview with Lee Kuan Yew, Istana, Singapore, 1993; and Michael Sherraden, Discussion with Ann Wee, her residence in Singapore, 2016.

called "coffin money" — because the British did not want to assume the financial obligations of social insurance.[6] Most of the colonial era provident funds have since faded away, but CPF in Singapore is today the centrepiece of social policy. It has been purposefully shaped into a comprehensive asset-building social policy, which provides some degree of security and development for most Singaporean families.

Asset-building policy innovations

The first policy innovation was to make CPF funds available for homeownership starting in 1968. Intertwined with the CPF today are many policies for housing, community development, healthcare, education, and various forms of insurance and investment.[7] Together, these comprise Singapore's core approach to household social protection and economic development. Singapore has created a new social policy system that has asset building as its central structure. Recent innovations extend asset building early in the life cycle. These include Edusave, the Baby Bonus, Child Development Accounts (CDAs), and related asset-building incentives, top-ups, and programmes. Although not all of these policy innovations are part of the CPF *per se*, they can be viewed as part of the same policy system. Space here does not permit a full assessment of CPF, but several themes are particularly important and discussed below.

Housing ownership

The Housing Development Board (HDB) in Singapore oversees shelter for about 80% of the population, with only 5% of these dwellings

---

[6] John Dixon, *National provident funds: The enfant terrible of social security* (International Fellowship for Social and Economic Development, 1989); and Michael Sherraden, Sudha Nair, S Vasoo, Ngiam Tee Liang and Margaret S. Sherraden, "Social policy based on assets: The impact of Singapore's Central Provident Fund", *Asian Journal of Political Science*, *3*(2), 112–133.

[7] Michael Sherraden, Sudha Nair, S Vasoo, Ngiam Tee Liang and Margaret S. Sherraden. "Social policy based on assets: The impact of Singapore's Central Provident Fund".

rented and the others owned by the occupant. No other public housing authority in the world emphasises homeownership to this extent. What is the purpose? The mission of HDB is primarily social. Although not usually emphasised, HDB and other government programmes substantially subsidise homeownership at the bottom, often combined with problem solving and support services, with the goal of creating stability for as many Singaporean families as possible. Overall, success in housing stability is noteworthy. As leading social worker Dr. Sudha Nair observes: "In Singapore, housing policy *is* social policy." (For a more thorough assessment of housing and asset building, see the chapter by Hongbo Jia and S Vasoo in this volume.)

Homeownership as a counter-balance to income inequality

As with many countries in the 21st century, income inequality in Singapore is high, and this is a very serious challenge. However, the Singapore government is strongly in the business of supporting asset accumulation, and family and community stability across the population. As noted above, most low-income Singapore households own their HDB flat, and flats have appreciated in value. Therefore, overall net worth for low-income families may be a meaningful positive sum, even if the major asset is not liquid. These families are strained, but they have a basic stability. (As a comparison, a larger percentage of low-income U.S. households do not own a home, have negative net worth, and experience housing insecurity.) If assets provide long-term stability for families, and enable a leg up for the next generation, then widespread homeownership can be a foundation for social protection and economic development over time, even among households with limited income. (See also the chapter in this volume by Irene Y.H. Ng.)

Community stability

Related to HDB housing policies is the important role of community design and organisation. 'Public housing' and community life are relatively stable in Singapore. Housing estates include blocks with all sizes of flats, so that the poorest families are not all concentrated in certain parts of the city. Indeed, there is no large area of substandard housing in Singapore, no large community that is considered dysfunctional, and no part of the country that could be called a ghetto or slum. In sum, social stability through well-constructed, secure, and owned housing — organised in functioning communities with easy access to services — is the basis of Singapore's development.[8]

Social development

This stability enables Singaporeans to weather periods of low income and other disruptions, with a greater likelihood of avoiding sudden moves and keeping their children in school. Social and economic policies are intertwined, and sometimes are the same policy (e.g., consider the CPF and HDB housing). Investment in social development, i.e., improving capacities, is emphasised over social maintenance, i.e., getting along (one summary is in Ngoh Tiong Tan and Kalyani Mehta's monograph[9] and see the chapter on social investments in this volume by Vasoo, which details additional policies for social development).

Ethnic and religious respect

As indicated above, Singapore as a nation was born amongst ethnic/religious strife and bloodshed, which in many ways were not separable from its geopolitical challenges. As a response, the government was immediately proactive on this issue, for both internal and external reasons. Today, Singaporean leadership remains committed to a 'multiracial society' and this shapes many aspects of social policy. Ethnic, cultural, and religious tolerance is consciously practised in Singapore. Quotas in HDB estates ensure that ethnic and religious groups are not separated from each other. Celebration of different backgrounds, religions, holidays, food, and languages is richer in

---

[8] Aline K. Wong and Stephen H.K. Yeh (eds.), *Housing a nation: 25 years of public housing in Singapore* (Singapore: Housing Development Board, 1985).

[9] Ngoh Tiong Tan and Kalyani Mehta (eds.), *Extending frontiers: Social issues and social work in Singapore* (Singapore: Eastern Universities Press, 2002).

Singapore than in most other countries. While racial and religious differences are always a challenge, the strong commitment to a 'multiracial society' — articulated by Lee Kuan Yew even before independence — is a lived experience in Singapore. The results are not perfect. People may have their ethic biases; some ethnicities may be over-represented in the lower-income population; and some areas of private housing may not be so well integrated. But policies and social practices aim strongly for mutual respect and appreciation, avoidance of inter-group conflict, and achieving as much educational and economic success as possible for all families regardless of ethnicity or religion (see the chapter by Vasoo in this volume).

Healthcare

The longevity of the Singaporean population is relatively high, and the cost for healthcare is relatively low, currently something like 5% of GDP. We can compare this to the United States, where life expectancy is about five years lower than in Singapore, yet healthcare expenditures are approaching 18% of GDP. To be sure, health policy is a very complex topic, with insufficient space to explore here. Of note for this chapter, MediSave, one of the schemes of the CPF, is an asset-building approach to certain aspects of healthcare, which may achieve some cost efficiencies.

Intergenerational fairness and sound political economy

Although little discussed, the asset-building policies of Singapore are also a bulwark against intergenerational unfairness, because each generation accumulates resources to fund its own social support and development. The system is to accumulate resources in advance rather than passing obligations for payment long into the future. The primary focus on asset building, along with the Singaporean policy objective of balanced public budgets, ensures that each generation lives within its means. For the most part, money is not borrowed and spent, leaving neither debt nor future obligation to the next generations. This policy has practical and moral effects that are positive across generations. In addition, the effects on the long-term political economy are noteworthy, reducing risk of macroeconomic blunders due to public indebtedness, and keeping options open for future generations to respond to the challenges of their own time without the burdens of paying for the past.

Social Policy Options and Mechanisms

To understand the 'lay of the land' in social policy, it may be useful to stand back to summarise key social policy options and mechanisms. These are:

Public provision to all, which includes:

(1) Institutions for social functioning (e.g., governments, laws, social protections, public health);
(2) Public goods provided for all (e.g., roads, schools, parks, transport).

Income support to households (called 'defined benefit'), which includes:

(1) Means-tested benefits payments or services to the poorest;
(2) Social insurance, with contributions during work life (in many countries, for unemployment, retirement, healthcare, and other provisions);
(3) Regular and inclusive income payments (e.g., monthly child allowances).

Asset building in households (called 'defined contribution'), which includes:

(1) Assets in the form of home equity, subsidised by direct or tax benefits;
(2) Savings for retirement and/or other purposes, perhaps matched or subsidised by tax benefits (e.g., retirement saving plans in many countries);

(3) Inclusive and lifelong asset building for multiple purposes, with some degree of progressive public subsidies (the policy concept in this chapter).

These social policy options and mechanisms are not mutually exclusive. Social policy in every nation is a complex mixture of these three themes. The point of discernment is not in policy purity, but rather in policy emphasis and interactions. For our purposes here, these themes and mechanisms may serve the purpose of placing inclusive asset-building policy in context.

Direct public provision to all

Regarding direct public provision to all in the form of social institutions and public goods, a case can be made that this theme of social policy is fundamental — indeed, it is the long-term pathway of what we call 'civilization'. Notwithstanding historical swings in ideology and politics, and large differences among societies, over long centuries of human development, more and more functions have been taken 'under wing' as social institutions and public goods, and then are quickly taken for granted. This list includes much of infrastructure, utilities, public health, knowledge building, education, social protections, transportation, communication, and so on. Almost all of these achievements result from social innovations — in conceptualisation, provision, organisation, and delivery — and serve major social development purposes, they are not usually discussed as 'social policy'. Nevertheless, this area of policy will likely continue to be the major pathway of social advancement for human societies.[10]

Income support to households

Most of 'social policy' provided directly to households is in the category of income support, or defined benefit (referring to a regular payment or

---

[10] Full consideration of social institutions and public goods as a major form of 'social policy' is a much larger discussion — and I believe a very important one — but it must wait for another day.

benefit amount). Income — as a proxy for consumption — has been the standard definition of poverty and well-being in 20th-century 'welfare states' and this definition has largely shaped public policy in almost all developed nations. For the most part, income support policies go to those who do not have sufficient income from labor market sources due to disability, unemployment, retirement, and other categorical conditions.

Asset building for households

An asset-building policy is not designed to support consumption in the short term but rather promote the accumulation of social investments over time. Thus, asset-based policy has a different logic and purpose — it is more about development than maintenance. Most nations have at least some degree of asset-building policy, typically operating through tax benefits, but often these are not inclusive. Tax benefits for retirement funds and homeownership in Singapore are also regressive, but the government as a counter-measure subsidises homeownership directly for low-income households with price subsidies and supports some on-going costs. Occasional top-ups and other mechanisms add to CPF balances for everyone. Altogether, Singapore, through the CPF and HDB, may be the most advanced instance of using public subsidies to bring a large portion of lower-income populations into asset building.

In the United States, current asset-based policies support home-ownership and retirement savings. Others support college savings and health savings. All of these have emerged during the past few decades and all are highly regressive.[11] The policy project of inclusive asset

---

[11] Susan Dynarski, "Who benefits from the education saving incentives? Income, educational expectations and the value of the 529 and Coverdell", *National Tax Journal*, 57(2), pp. 359–383, 2004; and C. Eugene Steuerle, Benjamin H. Harris, Signe-Mary McKernan, Caleb Quakenbush and Caroline Ratcliffe, *Who benefits from asset-building tax subsidies?* (Opportunity and Ownership Initiative Fact Sheet) (Washington, D.C.: Urban Institute, September 2014). Retrieved from Urban Institute website: http://www.urban.org/sites/default/files/alfresco/publication-pdfs/413241-Who-Benefits-from-Asset-Building-Tax-Subsidies-.PDF

building was defined in *Assets and the Poor*[12] and has made some progress in demonstrations and research evidence. The concept of 'inclusive asset building' has entered policy discourse, but it has a very long way to go to become a significant social policy theme and mechanism in the United States and most other countries.

Why Inclusive Asset Building?

Income support may not be a sufficient policy to achieve social stability

Income is the typical metric for evaluating economic well-being. The flow of resources over time supports consumption, but it may not be sufficient for well-being. Assets — the 'stock' of resources — enable people to finance irregular expenses, purchase large-ticket items, and weather financial crises.

Changing labour markets in 21st-century information and service economies are leading to rising income and asset inequality. Yet most social policies in existence today were designed during the 20th century for the industrial era. The underlying assumption has been that most households will be supported by wages from industrial labour markets, and defined benefit policy will fill the gaps — for the old, the disabled, death of a wage earner, and so on. However, this may no longer be the case for millions of households in advanced economies.

Two factors are critical: (1) increased globalisation and international competition that overall puts pressure on income from employment, and (2) information age technology is eliminating jobs and may eliminate many more in the years ahead. As a result of these trends, labour income is less adequate and less stable. Indeed, worldwide, a declining proportion of total economic product is going to labour, and growing portion is going to capital. This large

---

[12] Michael Sherraden, *Assets and the poor: A new American welfare policy* (New York: M.E. Sharpe, 1991).

pattern of resource flows has greatly exacerbated income and asset inequality.[13] To summarise succinctly, the assumption that labour income can and will support the well-being of most households is increasingly tenuous. Thus, it makes sense that more countries today are exploring alternatives, including the potential of asset-based social policy.[14]

Asset building can contribute to household development

For families to develop, it is necessary to accumulate resources for investments in education, skills, property, and enterprise. This is true for all families, rich and poor alike. Asset building creates material conditions, as well as outlooks and behaviours that promote house-hold stability and development.[15] Assets enable people to make invest-ments that expand their capabilities and improve their circumstances over the long term — for example, investments in education, homes, or enterprise.[16] The capacity to invest in one's self and one's family has become even more important in today's rapidly changing knowledge-based global economy.[17]

Assets are important because they provide resources and secu-rity for daily living, and serve as a form of insurance by enabling people to weather crises and meet irregular expenses. Assets also enable people to invest in education, homes, small businesses, and

---

[13] Thomas Piketty, *Capital in the twenty-first century* (Harvard University Press, Cambridge, MA, 2014).

[14] Organisation for Economic Co-operation and Development, *Asset building and the escape from poverty: A new welfare policy debate* (Washington, D.C., 2003).

[15] Michael Sherraden, *Assets and the poor: A new American welfare policy*.

[16] Will Paxton, "The asset-effect: An overview", in John Bynner and Will Paxton (eds.), *The asset-effect* (pp. 1–16) (London, England: Institute for Public Policy Research, 2001).

[17] Michael Sherraden, "Asset building research and policy: Pathways, progress, and potential of a social innovation", in Reid Cramer and Trina R. Williams Shanks (eds.), *The assets perspective: The rise of asset building and its impact on social policy* (pp. 263–284) (New York: Palgrave Macmillan, 2014).

other opportunities that support development over the long term.[18] There is widespread belief and a growing body of evidence that holding assets changes a person's attitudes and behaviours in positive ways. Many studies now show that financial assets and homeownership are positively associated with children's educational attainment and emotional and behavioural well-being, probably at least in part because assets change expectations about the future.[19] A growing body of research documents that early investments in children can have a large economic payoff[20] and Singapore is providing global leadership in asset-building policies for investments in children.[21]

---

[18] Michael Sherraden, *Assets and the poor: A new American welfare policy*; Michael Sherraden, "Asset building research and policy: Pathways, progress, and potential of a social innovation".

[19] Trina R. Williams Shanks, Youngmi Kim, Vernon Loke and Mesmin Destin, "Assets and child well-being in developed countries", *Children and Youth Services Review*, *32*(11), pp. 1488–1496, 2010; William Elliott, III and Sondra G. Beverly, "Staying on course: The effects of savings and assets on the college progress of young adults", *American Journal of Education*, *117*(3), pp. 343–374, 2011; Yunju Nam, Youngmi Kim, Margaret M. Clancy, Robert Zager and Michael Sherraden, "Do Child Development Accounts promote account holding, saving, and asset accumulation for children's future? Evidence from a statewide randomized experiment", *Journal of Policy Analysis and Management*, *32*(1), pp. 6–33, 2013; Jin Huang, Michael Sherraden, Youngmi Kim and Margaret M. Clancy, "Effects of Child Development Accounts on early social-emotional development: An experimental test", *JAMA Pediatrics*, *168*(3), pp. 265–271, 2014; Youngmi Kim, Michael Sherraden, Jin Huang and Margaret M. Clancy, "Child Development Accounts and parental educational expectations for young children: Early evidence from a statewide social experiment", *Social Service Review*, *89*(1), pp. 99–137, 2015; and Michael Sherraden, Margaret M. Clancy, Yunju Nam, Jin Huang, Youngmi Kim and Sondra G. Beverly, *et al.*, "Universal accounts at birth: Building knowledge to inform policy", *Journal of the Society for Social Work and Research*, 6, pp. 541–564, 2015.

[20] James J. Heckman and Dimitriy V. Masterov, *The productivity argument for investing in young youth* (Cambridge, MA: National Bureau of Economic Research, 2007).

[21] Vernon Loke and Michael Sherraden, "Building assets from birth: A global comparison of Child Development Account policies", *International Journal of Social Welfare*, *18*(2), pp. 119–129, 2009.

In the larger picture, there is growing recognition that income alone is insufficient to provide for well-being, even economic well-being.[22] Amartya Sen (1993) and others are looking towards capabilities. Asset-based policy can be seen as part of this larger discussion, as one strategy to build long-term capabilities. As public policy, asset building may be a form of 'social investment'.[23] From this perspective, inclusive asset-based policy is not a trade-off, but rather a complement to income-based policy.

Vision of Inclusive Asset-Based Policy

In contrast to a limited and very regressive asset-based policy currently in place in the United States, for example, comprehensive asset-building policy would be universal, progressive, and lifelong.[24]

Universal

Under *universal* policy everyone is 'in'. We have shown that full inclusion cannot be achieved without automatic enrollment and automatic deposits that are not contingent upon family deposits. If participation is voluntary, requiring people to actively enroll, a higher proportion of advantaged families will participate and benefit. If asset accumulation depends primarily on family deposits, advantaged families will receive nearly all of the subsidies (in current U.S. policy, more than

---

[22] Amartya Sen, "Capability and well-being", in Martha Nussbaum and Amartya Sen (eds.), *The quality of life* (pp. 30–53) (Oxford, England: Clarendon Press, 1993).

[23] James Midgley, "Growth, redistribution, and welfare: Toward social investment", *Social Service Review*, 73(1), pp. 3–21, 1999; Michael Sherraden, *Assets and the poor: A new American welfare policy*; and Michael Sherraden, "From social welfare state to social investment state", *Shelterforce: Journal of Affordable Housing and Community Building*, March/April, 16–18, 19, 29, 2003.

[24] Michael Sherraden, *Assets and the poor: A new American welfare policy*; Michael Sherraden, "Asset building research and policy: Pathways, progress, and potential of a social innovation".

90% of the subsidies go to the top 50% by income.[25] In contrast, automatic enrollment (with the ability to opt out) and automatic deposits extend the benefits of asset holding and asset subsidies to everyone, regardless of socioeconomic status. Key research and theory now inform this policy design.[26] In fact, in research on CDAs in the United States, automatic features have larger positive impacts on disadvantaged families.[27]

Progressive

Under *progressive* policy, the poor would receive greater public support than the non-poor. Good governance might define policy for the people who most need the support and services (disability benefits for the disabled, retirement support for older adults, and so on). In current asset-building policy in the United States, however, we do just the opposite, making the rich richer. At a minimum public policy should be *fair* (in this case, the same dollar amount for all). Ideally, policy would be *progressive* (more for those who are most in need).

Lifelong

Finally, under *lifelong* asset-building policy, investment accounts would be opened early — ideally at birth — and would follow

---

[25] C. Eugene Steuerle, Benjamin H. Harris, Signe-Mary McKernan, Caleb Quakenbush and Caroline Ratcliffe, *Who benefits from asset-building tax subsidies?* (Opportunity and Ownership Initiative Fact Sheet).

[26] Brigitte C. Madrian and Dennis F. Shea, "The power of suggestion: Inertia in 401(k) participation and savings behaviour", *The Quarterly Journal of Economics*, *116*, pp. 1149–1187, 2001; James J. Choi, David Laibson and Brigitte C. Madrian, "Plan design and 401(k) savings outcomes", *National Tax Journal*, *57*, pp. 275–298, 2004; and Sondra G. Beverly, Michael Sherraden, Reid Cramer, Trina R. Williams Shanks, Yunju Nam and Min Zhan, "Determinants of asset holdings", in Signe-Marie McKernan and M. Sherraden (eds.), *Asset building and low-income families* (pp. 89–151) (Washington, D.C.: Urban Institute, 2008).

[27] Youngmi Kim, Michael Sherraden, Jin Huang and Margaret M. Clancy, "Child Development Accounts and parental educational expectations for young children: Early evidence from a statewide social experiment".

individuals into retirement. Opening accounts early is important for a number of reasons. Foremost, asset accumulation is a long-term process for most people. Over time, regular deposits — even small ones — can result in significant asset accumulation. Opening accounts and providing subsidies early also enables families to benefit from investment earnings so assets may grow substantially even if families do not contribute. Since the early 2000s, Singapore has moved in this direction with asset building for children in the Baby Bonus, CDAs, and other schemes. Conceptually, these policy schemes are related to the CPF, and indeed unused child and youth balances roll over into the CPF in adulthood. The United States is also making progress towards this ideal, with some U.S. states and cities now opening accounts for all children.[28]

Some Challenges for Inclusive Asset Building in Singapore

Social policies everywhere face continual challenges due to changing social conditions, economic pressures and opportunities, and demographic trends. Policies must continually adapt to be relevant and effective. Asset-building policy of Singapore is no exception. In the following sub-sections, as examples, we consider three of these challenges.

Aging population

Along with many other countries, Singapore has a rapidly aging population, and this demographic transition poses large challenges for social policy. Older adults in Singapore developed along with the nation. They worked hard and helped to build the new nation, but

---

[28] V Vernon Loke and Michael Sherraden, "Building assets from birth: A global comparison of Child Development Account policies"; and Michael Sherraden, Margaret M. Clancy, Yunju Nam, Jin Huang, Youngmi Kim and Sondra G. Beverly, *et al.*, "Universal accounts at birth: Building knowledge to inform policy".

early in life they did not earn much money. For this group, most of their CPF savings have gone into mortgage payments. Therefore, most older Singaporeans own their HDB flat, but many have low incomes and may lack sufficient liquidity to cover living expenses. This is a good example of the need for policy flexibility, and the government has responded in recent years with a Pioneers Scheme and a Silver Support Scheme, which provide additional income and other supports for older adults. In addition, there is now an option for a reverse mortgage to monetise home equity while guaranteeing residential stability. Other policy innovations may be required. In the longer term, this challenge may abate because younger generations have higher real incomes, and they are more likely to inherit housing wealth, so their economic circumstances during old age may be more comfortable. However, given the potential for greater extensions in average lifespan, the challenge of an aging population will remain unpredictable.

Technological transformations in money and financial services

Turning to transformations in money and financial services, it now seems possible, even likely, that 'money' as a medium of exchange will disappear and transactions of all kinds will be tallied electronically as a unit of account. Financial services will be radically transformed in this process, decentralised, and delivered to everyone via cell phone or other mobile technology. The CPF and its cousin schemes can adapt to these changes, and indeed benefit from them.[29] This new era of money and financial services will be highly efficient and, due to low costs, has the potential to be fully inclusive. In this technological environment, the CPF and other asset-building schemes can move even

---

[29] The CPF has kept relatively 'up to date' in applications of information technology. Singapore in 1962 was among the first nations to computerise its social security system, and there is an on-going emphasis on participants interacting with CPF on-line, increasingly from mobile devices. The transition to a cashless society is likely to continue CPF's proactive technological history.

more towards universal social institutions providing their services as 'public goods'. I have already noticed in Singapore that more people take the CPF for granted over time — it has become part of the background, as if such policy were as normal as running water in every home or transport for all on the Mass Rapid Transit (MRT). While not easy to imagine today, it could be in the future that all financial affairs, including asset building, will happen automatically for everyone, with minimal requirements to plan or 'behave' by individuals. There will be different interpretations of this future, but in my view, transforming all of finance into a 'public good' holds great positive potential.

Long-term protection of accumulated assets

Singapore can be commended for its commitment to 'pre-funding' many social obligations in the form of individual accounts, along with a growing list of public endowments for specific purposes. As noted, this provides a degree of macroeconomic stability and avoids the problem of passing large debts to future generations. At the same time, the significant accumulation of assets for public policy presents a challenge — to be sure, this is a good challenge to have, but nonetheless a serious one. Not every nation has the ability to manage a large asset accumulation successfully. Where governments lack abilities or integrity, assets can be depleted by error or inefficiency, macroeconomic mismanagement (especially inflation), or outright corruption. Indeed, this is what happened to most of the colonial era provident funds.[30] Even in advanced and democratic nations, there is a significant risk that elected officials will vote to spend accumulated money for some near-term purposes — and to get re-elected. How has Singapore handled this challenge? The answer is a little complex, but involves large sums invested outside the country, overseen by a few public authorities and managers in Singapore. The President has been entrusted with power of holding the 'key' to these asset accumulations, a mechanism designed to prevent the problems listed

---

[30] John Dixon, *National provident funds: The enfant terrible of social security.*

earlier on. So far, Singapore's presidents have been of very high quality, with vision and backbone, and have fulfilled this responsibility.[31] But what about the future? How long can Singapore depend on good governance, capable and fully honest, to manage large asset accumulations? What will happen if leadership mistakes eventually occur? Are there enough eyes and enough voices to counteract a leadership failure? Without doubt, Singaporean officials are aware of this long-term risk. Policy options that might reduce this long-term risk include greater use of large global asset managers, individualisation of assets (direct ownership and control) in accounts of CPF participants, and/or more systematic external review in some form. It seems likely that one or more of these or other protective mechanisms may put in place over time.

Overall, the asset-building policies defined by the CPF and its cousin schemes are a noteworthy achievement, playing a key role in strengthening families and communities and in building the nation. Not every country can say this about its social policies. At the same time, as emphasised in this chapter, no human endeavour is ever without challenges.

Turning to the larger discussion of Singapore's asset-building policies, we can explore a number of different pathways and specific policy areas. In this book the excellent contributors take us on this journey, with careful assessments and practical insights. These inquiries and observations can be useful both for Singaporeans and for scholars and policy makers in other nations.

---

[31] I have known one of these presidents, Mr. S.R. Nathan. He started his career as a social worker and was the longest-serving president of Singapore. His attention to social policy in Singapore is apparent in many of his writings. I was honored to be the inaugural S.R. Nathan Professor at National University of Singapore, and fortunate to enjoy several long discussions with Mr. Nathan before his death in 2016.

Chapter 2

Investments for Social Sector to Tackle Some Key Social Issues

S Vasoo

Introduction

By the next Singapore 100 (SG100), there will be some key emerging social issues which will need special attention and require new social innovative approaches for human capital development. More future social investments in terms of fund allocation, deployment of better qualified and committed social service personnel, improved facilities, enlarging volunteer base, value adding social policies and outreach service delivery can be deployed earlier to the social sectors to act as social antibodies to build the resilience of vulnerable working-class families who may slip down the ladder to achieve their human potential. We can no longer label the deployment of social and financial resources as welfarist because the focus will be on development of socioeconomic and psychological potential of working-class families with children and other vulnerable groups who face difficulty to cope with increasing cost escalation in meeting the demands to cope with their livelihood. This working-class sector of the Singapore population is not small and comprises of the 1st to the 50th decile household groups who are motivated to improve but face constraints beyond their social control to better their lives which in turn do have impact on their children's future. To simply put it, they are people who are employed but these individuals do not earn sufficient wages to help them tide over a sustainable period of time. Similarly, these households find it tough to enable their children to acquire relevant skills to prepare them to be productive and be future ready for a more competitive global economy. The average monthly income of these household groups is between S$494 and S$2,155[1] and most of them live in one- to three-room public flats. These affected families are more likely to face marginal growth in income because of new disruptive economies and the effects of increasing competitive wages from emerging economies in the region. The workers in the labour-intensive and manufacturing sectors and the older middle-level management, professional and technical employees are likely to face economic and social setbacks.

The inability to be versatile in analysing the emerging social issues and the outcome of the service delivery in the social sectors can prevent social policy makers to acquire better insight to anticipate social issues for effective management of social problems, resources and services.[2] Social analytics skills will be required if administrators can play a meaningful role in community problem solving in the coming years. At this juncture, there are lots of information available from the private, non-governmental and governmental sectors but these are kept under close private purview and not shared or coordinated. There is a wealth of information in the private and public archives that could be shared for more effective community problem solving. Unless there is a cooperative spirit of sharing of data for finding better solutions to deal with new social and economic challenges, we will be no better in the long run as the data gather dust and the societal issues are less innovatively dealt with. With the saying "old wines in new bottles", the approach and solution will be more or less the same.

---

[1] Department of Statistics Singapore, *Yearbook of statistics* (Singapore: The Author, 2015).

[2] S Vasoo, "New directions of community development in Singapore", in Ngoh Tiong Tan and Kalyani Mehta (eds.), *Extending frontiers: Social issues and social work in Singapore* (pp. 20–36) (Singapore: Eastern University Press, 2002).

Social Challenges and Social Investments

There are some major social issues that policy makers must keep a keen eye on and these require the employment of social analytics to appreciate how social issues will surface and their impacts on the socioeconomic and political landscape of Singapore. In having a good grasp on the emerging social issues, policy makers will then be able to plan realistic and realisable social programmes to tackle them. Attempts will be made in this paper to touch on some major issues that are likely to emerge. The case for further social investments to act as social antibodies in the context of Singapore is advocated to build and strengthen the social capital of those vulnerable families living in 292,344 units of one- to three-room public housing flats. This accounts for about 30.2% of the total number of 968,856 flats of various room types allocated to families in the various Housing and Development Board (HDB) estates.[3] The People's Action Party (PAP) government having decently housed almost about 82% of Singapore's population[4] to live in good public housing which is a landmark international record, must get HDB to re-examine its role of not just dwelling only on estate management,[5] but also place more emphasis on its role in social management by initiating the setting up of a social management unit in each HDB Branch to identify at the frontline vulnerable families for follow-up support in concert with Family Service Centres (FSCs) and other community and social service organisations. The challenge will be for HDB to find how it can also deal with the emerging social issues facing the major bulk of vulnerable families living in the HDB heartland. Identifying the factors that make vulnerable families fall through the social crack will be useful for various social and community organisations to strengthen the capacity of vulnerable families. Any early intervention efforts such as education, finance, accessibility to social services,

---

[3] Housing and Development Board, *HDB Annual Report 2014/15* (Singapore, 2015).
[4] Housing and Development Board, *HDB Annual Report 2014/15*.
[5] Beng Huat Chua, "Navigating between limits: The future of public housing in Singapore", *Housing Studies*, *29*(4), pp. 520–533, 2014.

employability, health enhancement and skills development, can help towards levelling up these families and prevent serious social and economic divisions in Singapore society.[6]

Meeting Issues Facing Working Class Families and Implications

During the last decade, Singapore society is seeing a widening income gap and there is a sector of new poor being trapped in low wage due to depressed salaries arising from imported cheap labour and low skills.[7] This sector of the population requires closer attention because the children of these families are likely to be disadvantaged as they will not be able to acquire the numeracy and literacy levels required to start them off in primary schooling. This is because parents do not have the educational capacity to prepare their children who are normal but not educationally ready in numeracy and literacy to level up with their counterparts whose parents are more educated or schooled. These new poor families have both family and social difficulties which unless addressed early can lead to various social breakdowns. Here, the FSCs can work in concert with various community groups with the support of the Ministry of Education (MOE) and Ministry of Social and Family Development (MSF) to initiate early social and educational intervention programmes such as family mentoring, counseling, family life education, educational head start, care networks, income supplement projects and early reading. When more children in the low-income families are reached out to benefit from early supportive education and literacy programs, they will be better prepared for schooling to develop their potential. The community and policy makers can assist by allocating more resources to militate against the loss

---

[6] Kwong Ping Ho, "Towards a more equal, self-reliant society", in Soon Hock Kang and Chan-Hoong Leong (eds.), *Singapore perspectives 2012: Singapore inclusive: Bridging divides* (pp. 101–107) (Singapore: World Scientific Publishing, 2012).

[7] Irene Y.H. Ng, "Multi-stressed low-earning families in contemporary policy context: Lessons from Work Support recipients in Singapore", *Journal of Poverty, 17*(1), pp. 86–109, 2013.

of opportunities to enable many low-income children who otherwise may become ill-equipped to benefit from education and skills training opportunities. In the longer term, the social divide can be further widened when more of low-income children fail to acquire the knowledge and skills that can prepare them to earn a livelihood not only in Singapore but also globally. When the social gap widens, the consequences will not be good for the Singapore community as a divided community may be socially unhealthy to Singapore with more frustrated intergenerational younger families.[8]

The Gini coefficient based on per household member after taking into account of government transfers is 0.412.[9] This income gap can widen further in the future when wages get depressed. One of the more serious consequences for not tackling the income divide will be the confounding effects of ethnicity and low income. Therefore, policy makers must be sensitive to moderate the economic market to reduce the widening social divisions in our Singapore society.[10] There must be more visible hand of the government to moderate and implement some effective forms of redistributive justice with an economic heart, particularly in education, healthcare, housing and workfare for lower skilled workers.[11] Unless members of the public feel the impact in their social and economic lives, current policy makers will lose their credence and more contending policy opinion makers will surface to provide other populist options for the working class. As a consequence, there will be more social fractures within the society and these can cause social disruptions and dis-welfare in the community, and worse translating into ethnic tensions and conflicts.

---

[8] Irene Y.H. Ng, "Being poor in a rich 'Nanny State': Developments in Singapore social welfare", in Linda Y.C. Lim (eds.), *Singapore's Economic Development, Retrospection and Reflections* (pp. 279–297) (Singapore: World Scientific Publishing, 2016).

[9] Department of Statistics Singapore, *Yearbook of statistics 2015*.

[10] Nurhidayah Hassan, *Developing an analytical framework on social cohesion in Singapore: Reflections from the framing of social cohesion debates in the OECD and Europe* (Singapore, EU Centre, 2013).

[11] Azad Latif, *Hearts of resilience: Singapore's Community Engagement Programme* (Singapore: Institute of Southeast Asian Studies, 2011).

Social workers and social sector professionals can engage families in the low-income group to participate in early educational start-up programmes which can enable the children to be more numerate and literate. Early start-up programmes targeted at two to four years old at community levels supported by concerted and coordinated efforts of various community self-help groups such as Singapore Indian Development Association (SINDA), Yayasan Mendaki, Chinese Development Assistance Council (CDAC), NTUC My First Skool and PAP Community Foundation (PCF), can help reach out sooner to stimulate their early learning interest. Also, family matched saving projects involving low-income families to become more financially literate and be better motivated to upgrade their skills could be implemented at the local community level as this programme will be more accessible to them. Where needed, group boarding centres in the neighbourhood can be initiated particularly to cater for the young who are prone to parental neglect and care and be made easily accessible to their parents.

Addressing Skills Training Issues

With globalisation, it is envisaged that Singapore like other developed economies, will be confronted with more competition from developing economies with both skilled and unskilled manpower for market share of products and services. This situation will be inevitable and the likelihood is that wages are going to be depressed as the offers by the developing world will be cheaper, efficient and effective. So, to meet such challenging scenario, Singapore has limited options but to take steps to train every young child and person up the higher economic value chain in market products and services such as marine and biological sciences, medicine and pharmacy, chemical and nano-technology, food safety and production, precision and aeronautical engineering, building and housing construction, and environmental and water resource technology. Human service professionals can help organise family life, self-help and community education programmes that will kick start interest among low-income parents to know about community resources and how they can tap them for their betterment. Many more children from low-income households can be helped through such early socio-educational intervention projects to realise their human potential and skills to work in globalised industries and workplaces. A more challenging option will be to start a few boarding schools under enterprise models for children with fractured family life as well as very low-income families. The boarding school environment will be nurturing and supportive for them to learn appropriate social and life skills and families can opt voluntarily to participate in the scheme and have access to their children.

Dealing with the Issues of Silver Tsunami

As anticipated, there will be a beginning of the silver tsunami before 2025, where more families will be afflicted by the burdens in caring for their less mobile elderly parents.[12] This social burden will be more pronounced among dual career and young adult families and more so if they have terminally sick elderly parents. Besides social and economic costs, families may have to find more accessible social and daycare services. Along with this need for supportive care services, families will also face grief and loss of their elderly parents for which social care services to help family members cope with such emotions will be helpful. In response to the social, psychosocial and health consequences facing the greying elderly population,[13] personnel working in health and family service settings can play a role to help promote community care cooperatives and community hospice care services to support families with elderly needing different social care services and support.[14]

---

[12] David Chan, John Elliott, Gillian Koh, Lily Kong, Sudha Nair and Ern Ser Tan, *et al*, "Social capital and development", in Mui Teng Yap and Christopher Gee (eds.), *Population outcomes: Singapore 2050* (Singapore: Institute of Policy Studies, Lee Kuan Yew School of Public Policy, National University of Singapore, 2014).

[13] Lena L. Lim and Ee-Heok Kua, "Living alone, loneliness, and psychological well-being of older persons in Singapore", *Current Gerontology and Geriatrics Research*, 2(1), pp. 33–40, 2011.

[14] Angelique Chan, Chetna Malhotra, Rahul Malhotra and Truls Østbye, "Living arrangements, social networks and depressive symptoms among older men and

The rise in the many elderly needing healthcare and social service support will lead to debates on issues related to end life and the allocation of healthcare resources. Human service professionals will have to face such debates of Singapore society and prepare families with elderly persons to have plans before life ends. This is to ensure that one will have less traumatic troubles in living through the tertiary period of one's life. Therefore, it will be helpful if social agencies involved in elderly care can engage families at appropriate time in making end of life plans for elderly relatives in their frail years. Such preparations are critical as families will be better prepared to deal with issues of death and dying.

Many elderly will have long years to live after their mandatory retirement. In fact, the whole aspect of retirement has to be reviewed as the elderly of tomorrow will have much knowledge and expertise which can still be tapped to contribute socioeconomically to our society and it will be demeaning to let ageism dictate the working shelf life of the seniors. With declining population, retirement issue should deserve a relook and life-long working could be planned.[15] Our society must be graceful in valuing the seniors and find various ways to engage them in productive and meaningful activities.

Issues of Out-Sourcing to In-Sourcing

It is observed that there is an increasing trend by social and community sectors to outsource community activities. Why is the case? In the name of efficiency and the urgency for quick turnover, organisers and providers of services often face time constraints. Therefore most community activities are planned within a short time frame and often tied to the term of office holders. Such an emphasis can make volunteer groups or organisations insular and not development oriented.

women in Singapore", *International Journal of Geriatric Psychiatry*, *26*(6), pp. 630–639, 2011.

[15] Mui Teng Yap and Christopher Gee (2015), "Ageing in Singapore: Social issues and policy challenges", in David Chan (ed.), *50 Years of Social Issues in Singapore* (pp. 3–30) (Singapore: World Scientific Publishing, 2015).

They then become task- or activity-centred and slowly digress from being people-centred which is aimed at promoting self-help and community ownership of those who are beneficiaries of the community activities and social programmes. As such, many social and community organisations and volunteer groups adopt a less outreaching approach to understand the changing needs of the community. In the longer term, such a move will make them more detached from keeping in touch with the needs of people who are uninvolved or are vulnerable to social problems.

Encountering Issues of Centralisation of Leadership

The leadership in social and community organisations is greying and more attention should be devoted to encourage and enlist resourceful younger residents to help manage them. Many community organisations have become gerontocratic and can be less responsive to the changing needs of the neighbourhoods. In the making, they can become senior citizen clubs which will only meet one specific group of the resident population, namely the elderly. So far, punctuated attempts have been made to renew the leadership and these are unlikely to rejuvenate community organisations.

It is observed that the rate participation of lower-income households and minorities is not as significant and this could be due to the less tangible benefits offered by the programmes delivered by community groups and organisations. The participation of both minorities and lower-income families are critical in maintaining social cohesion and community bonding. Hence, more concrete services to meet their social and economic needs will address the public goods dilemma as this will reduce their cost for participation. When community organisations do not bear this in mind in their service delivery, both minorities and low-income households will not be motivated to participate in some mainstream community activities.

Another significant development in the older neighbourhoods of Singapore is the hollowing out of the more resourceful and younger residents. When this process accelerates, these neighbourhoods become eventually silver communities. This is also compounded by a higher outflow of the young to the exuberant facilities of other New Towns. It is envisaged that there will be depletion of social and leadership resources and these neighbourhoods are likely to slow down and become less attractive to new residents. Inevitability, social burdens for care will increase unless more community care services and support networks are encouraged through community development efforts.

Enhancing Self-Help and Community Ownership

There should be less outsourcing contracts and more in-sourcing activities by mobilising residents to forms not-for-profit organisations or social enterprises. Such attempts will provide more opportunities for residents to participate in decision making so that they can take ownership. Community care groups and support networks can be formed. This will make participants engage in problem solving instead of being passive recipients of services.[16] Community organisations widen the base of participation by residents forming various interest groups or task forces to work on several social issues and projects such as security watch and crime prevention, cooperative care services, improvements to recreational facilities, pollution control, thrift through micro-credit groups, and environmental enhancement causes. It will be useful where possible to encourage residents to take charge in finding more effective ways to deal with local matters and with the support of the Town Councils (TCs) and Community Development Councils (CDCs). This will truly be promoting community development as local residents will learn and find more realistic solutions to solve their specific needs and problems and become accountable for their decisions.

---

[16] Mohamad Maliki Bin Osman, "Social issues in developing a community in Singapore", in David Chan (ed.), *50 years of social issues in Singapore* (pp. 189–203) (Singapore: World Scientific Publishing, 2015).

However, with the move towards information technology, people could become impersonal and more homebound, social interactions could be reduced and social bonding could be threatened. Therefore, all the more personalised outreaching efforts have to be complemented with online contacts.

Rejuvenating Leadership and Organisational Renewal

It is also observed that a significant number of grassroots leaders of community organisations in the mature housing estates are about above 50 years old. These organisations face difficulties in recruiting younger residents to take up leadership. With the greying of the organisational leadership, there is urgency to rejuvenate the leadership of community organisations by attracting younger professionals to participate them. It is not just sufficient to recruit them but they must be mentored with some committed older leaders. With attachment to specific mentors, they can be anchored to the organisations and this will reduce attrition facing younger persons taking up leadership in organisations dominated by seniors. A rejuvenated leadership will continue to be vibrant and relevant to meet the needs and aspirations of younger generation of residents. We must also attract younger people-centred community leaders who must be given all the support to carry out community problem solving activities. People-centred community leaders are proactive and they should not be piled with so much tasks that they then suffer burnout. More importantly, the young leadership should be given management skills training to understand the needs of residents so that they can help make community organisations responsive to tackling emerging social needs.

Reaching out to Lower-Income Residents and Minorities

As Singapore is an increasingly globalised, open economy, it is inevitable the residents with low skills are likely to face depressed wages and this can lead to widening income gap. Singaporeans with better skills are likely to move ahead while those with low skills and less literacy in information technology will fall behind in income. Social stratification based on socioeconomic classes confounded by ethnicity may surface if excessive free market competition is not tempered.[17] As a consequence, social conflicts could emerge and when this is capitalised by political and racial fanatics, our community harmony and cohesion could be fractured. As such, community organisations like CDCs can take preventive measures to deliver community-based self-help programmes such as social and educational assistance, computer training, youth vocational guidance and counselling programmes, family-life and development activities, and continuing learning programmes to help the socially disadvantaged groups. As a long-term measure for people capability building, it is important to develop more re-skill training schemes.

There appears a re-emergence of ethnic ghettoes in one to two-room neighbourhoods and it must be addressed quickly by providing mixed room housing types (one- to three-room units). These social investment efforts can help to reduce the social frictions between classes and ethnic groups. Fanatics will find less temptation to exploit the race card as the problems facing low-income families appear across all ethnic groups. Hence, the realistic solution is to help level up the capabilities of all disadvantaged families despite their ethnicity.

Singapore is indeed a multiracial society comprising of Chinese (77.7%), Malays (14.1%), Indians (7.9%) and others (1.4%). It is crucial that various efforts both at the social policy and community activity levels, are consciously implemented to generate better racial understanding and where necessary to encourage multiracial involvement of residents and community leaders. To strengthen Singapore's social landscape, it is desirable to encourage multi-ethnic participation in social and recreation activities organised by grassroots organisations, civic and social organisations, TCs and CDCs. In the longer term,

---

[17] Paul Cheung, "Income growth and redistribution in Singapore: Issues and challenges", in Soon Hock Kang and Chan-Hoong Leong (eds.), *Singapore perspectives 2012: Singapore inclusive: Bridging divides* (pp. 7–22) (Singapore: World Scientific Publishing, 2012).

social harmony is critical to the socio-economic well-being of Singapore's communities of different ethnic backgrounds.

Renewal and Rejuvenation of Aging Neighbourhoods

It will be evident that in the next two decades, a number of silver neighbourhoods will appear. If attempts by the public housing authority to renew and rejuvenate these neighbourhoods are slower than population aging in these places, then these estates will become listless and socially rundown. Local social and economic activities will slow down and younger people will not be attracted to live in these neighbourhoods as seniors will dominate.[18] Ultimately there will be more families facing the need for care of elderly parents or relatives. As many of these households have working family members, they will face the burden of care.[19] Social breakdowns are likely without accessible social support and community care services delivered at the local level. Therefore, there will be demands for more community-based programmes to cater to the needs of families who have frail aged family members.[20] The number of such families is expected to increase from the next decade. In light of this situation, more community groups, voluntary welfare organisations together with the involvement of residents as well as hospitals, will have to work as partners to provide community care services such as home-help, meals service, daycare, integrated housing and community nursing.[21] Here, community care

---

[18] Im Sik Cho and Blaž Križnik, *Community-based urban development: Evolving urban paradigms in Singapore and Seoul* (New York: Springer, 2017).

[19] Lena L. Lim and Tze Pin Ng, "Living alone, lack of a confidant and psychological well-being of elderly women in Singapore: The mediating role of loneliness", *Asia-Pacific Psychiatry*, 2(1), pp.33–40, 2010.

[20] Keng Hua Chong, Wei Quin Yow, Debbie Loo and Ferninda Patrycia, "Psychosocial well-being of the elderly and their perception of matured estate in Singapore", *Journal of Housing for the Elderly*, 29(3), pp. 259–297, 2015.

[21] J. Ong, M. Lim and L. Seong, "The Singapore experience: Understanding the older persons who utilize community rehabilitation services", *International Journal of Integrated Care*, 13(8), 2013.

cooperatives could be formed to offer services which will be more convenient and accessible to the families with frail elderly needing care and attention. There is potential for this type of social enterprises to be established with participation of families as one of the stakeholders.

Preparing Personnel in Social Service Sector

The management curricula for social sector training should not be based on a parochial orientation namely emphasising a remedial management model. The curricula must fire the imagination of the human service professions to equip them the knowledge and skills to examine issues with a new perspective, challenge assumptions of our current management practice, and find new sets of management strategies in social service delivery. Imbibing eclectic management thinking is essential because in the social and economic sectors, competition has intensified as a result of slower growth and resource limitations. It is new ideas and innovations that will make social service delivery more effective. Therefore, human service professionals should be trained to have a development and outreaching focus and to deal at front end where there is wider client or consumer base rather than just sorting the small tail end of the problem which can be complicated. In short, more focus be directed at social development to prevent human problems rather than just dealing with people when brokered.

Conclusion

Social investment efforts must encourage people to taking ownership of the various social and economic activities which are delivered in the various neighbourhoods in partnership with a number of groups. To be impactful, social service organisations or groups cannot continue to assume that they know what residents want but to outreach to appraise their social needs or requirements. In short, social investments should in the due course promote self-help and the focus should be to encourage mutual help and not dependency and helplessness.

As community needs become more complex and challenging, there will an increase in interest groups which will lobby resource and policy holders to advance their group agenda. Therefore, leaders of social and community organisations will have to be more objective and work for the interest of the majority. For them to continue to be viable and effective, there must be active attempts to recruit, motivate and retain younger leaders who are committed to find ways to meet the interest of the wider good. Unless there are such committed social and community leaders, it will be more trying to fortify the social health of the community.

As Singapore becomes more globalised, social needs and problems are increasingly challenging to solve as they will require the efforts of a number of key players. Therefore, community problem solving will need the partnership of several parties. The partnership model of the government, community organisations and groups, corporate sector and philanthropic individuals can be encouraged as such model emphasises on the belief in sharing the social burdens. All partners involved in community problem solving have shared social responsibilities. Both manpower and matching grants are allocated to various projects to be carried out by community groups, social enterprises, non-profit sector and community organisations. The social consequences for not furthering social investments can cause social barriers and divisions and thereby precipitating the growing number of non-productive citizens who can be a liability to the society. Worse is that they become disruptive to the well-being of the community and more funds will be needed to habilitate them. Hence, social investments at an early stage of a person's life will make the society more vibrant.

Chapter 3

Singapore's Multiculturalism: An Asset for Nation Building

Norshahril Saat

Introduction

In 2008, the Singapore Police Force Band, the oldest marching band in the country,[1] was invited to perform at the Edinburgh Military Tattoo in Scotland. Its repertoire included Chinese, Malay, and Indian tunes. The performance also featured the lion dance, Indian drums, and a medley of Malay songs. Any Singaporean who watched the performance could easily identify with it, as it represents the country's multicultural character. Multiculturalism has become part of the country's official 'narrative' and Singaporeans accept the philosophy as one strengthening the nation rather than dividing it. The government has also laid out several Our-of-Bounds (OB) Markers to prevent the souring of race relations: for instance, members of a particular race cannot hurl words deem insulting to other communities' beliefs, customs, or diets. To be sure, the way Singaporeans understand multiculturalism has positive consequence for the country in the past and present. It safeguards minority rights, and prevents negative perceptions towards them. To date, the ideology has been successful in

---

[1] The Singapore Police Force Band was formed in 1925.

preventing *inter alia* Islamophobia, anti-Semitism and anti-Indian. Simultaneously, it has allowed greater appreciation between different religious and ethnic groups.

This chapter examines the ways the Singapore government manages ethnic relations which contribute to the country's relative peace over the years. It argues that the government's multicultural ideology, and the policies associated with it, help maintain the country's stability and harmonious relations among citizens. It also utilises the ideology to rationalise the country's administration and policies on race, use of public places and language policies.[2] Apart from applying soft approaches through promoting multiculturalism, the government also adopts robust policies and zero tolerance against those threatening the country's race relations. Furthermore, the ideology would not be sustainable without active participation of key stakeholders, non-governmental organisations (NGOs) and ordinary citizens, which cements the ideology as a Singapore way of life.

The chapter will be organised in the following ways. First, it highlights that multiculturalism remains a contested term because Western and Asian understanding of multiculturalism differ. In Singapore, different ethnic communities are allowed to practise their own religion, culture, and language, as long as they do not impinge on the common values supported by the government. How Singaporeans understand multiculturalism will be explained in the subsequent section. It looks at the history of the concept which dates back to colonial period and when Singapore was part of Malaysia between 1963 and 1965. This will be followed by analysing the impact of the government's multicultural policy on the country's state-and-society relations. This article concludes by pointing out the challenges of multiculturalism in the age of new media. After more than 50 years of nation building, ethnocentrism persists in Singapore. One can contend that multiculturalism should transcend from being a mechanism to prevent another racial riot to one that genuinely fosters good understanding and appreciation among different ethnic communities.

---

[2] Beng Huat Chua, "Multiculturalism in Singapore: An instrument of social control", *Race & Class*, 44(3), pp. 58–77, 2003, p. 76.

Multiple Versions of Multiculturalism

In a globalised world, there are no states that can be considered ethnically homogeneous. Almost all modern states today are made up of one or two dominant ethnic groups and many other sub-ethnic groups. For example, Singapore has 74% Chinese, 13% Malays, and 9% Indians. Malaysia consists of 68.6% *Bumiputeras* (inclusive of Malays), 23.4% Chinese, 7% Indians, and 1% of many other smaller communities.[3] It cannot be denied, however, that there are states with hundreds of sub-ethnic groups with no one dominant group. For example, Papua New Guinea has 900 spoken languages. Solomon Islands houses 70 languages even though it has a population of 500,000 people.[4]

To be sure, countries that claim to be multicultural will have to deal with three issues: minority nationalism, indigenous rights, and immigrant communities.[5] Multicultural states are often presented with this dilemma: how much should governments give in to majority interests without sacrificing minority rights? Most multicultural states adopt the principle of majority rules and minority rights. The ethnic group with the highest number of people assumes political power: they are the heads of state and prime ministers, dominate positions in the executive (cabinet), and control key appointments in the bureaucracy. They also control the resources and wealth of the country. The Chinese, being the majority in Singapore, occupy key government positions. Since independence, all three of the country's prime ministers are Chinese. The Chinese are appointed to key positions in the Cabinet. In Malaysia, the Malays/Muslims form the dominant ethnic

---

[3] Department of Statistics Malaysia, *Current population estimates, Malaysia, 2014–2016* (Putrajaya, Malaysia: The Author, 2016). Retrieved on 9 February 2017 from http://www.dosm.gov.my/v1/index.php?r=column/cthemeByCat&cat=155&bul_id=OWlxdE VoYlJCS0hUZzJyRUcvZEYxZz09&menu_id=L0pheU43NWJwRWVSZklWdzQ4Tlh UUT09

[4] Francis Fukuyama, *The origins of political order* (Great Britain: Profile Books, 2011), pp. xii–xiii.

[5] Will Kymlicka, "Liberal multiculturalism: Western models, global trends, and Asian debates", in Will Kymlicka and Baogang He (eds.), *Multiculturalism in Asia* (pp. 22–55) (Oxford, England: Oxford University Press).

group, and they occupy key political positions in the country. Since the country's independence in 1957, all six prime ministers have been Malays/Muslims.

On the other hand, multicultural states must ensure that their minorities are not relegated to the societal fringes. Minorities should be free to practice their culture and religion. Human rights groups also assess governments based on their track record in allowing freedom of expression, faith and culture. Good governance is also judged by the minority representation in the legislature and civil service. The Singapore government takes minority rights issue and rights seriously through the formation of the Presidential Council for Minority Rights.[6] The council's role is mainly to draw on public attention if there are any matters that may be of concern to minorities and serve as a check to Parliament whenever a new legislation affects minority interests. However, it does not have any powers to veto any legislation passed by Parliament. It also cannot review Money Bills or bills the Prime Minister certified as 'urgent'.[7] As at 2016, there are 16 members in the council including the chairman, six permanent members and nine ordinary members. The permanent members include Prime Minister Lee Hsien Loong and former Prime Minister Goh Chok Tong.

However, demographics alone does not determine power relations of a particular state. The Chinese in Malaysia, the Philippines, and Indonesia hold economic power even though they are minorities in these countries. In South Africa during the Apartheid era, the natives do not hold power, even though they are the majority; the country was led by the Whites.

Multiculturalism, as a governing ideology, is a way of balancing irreconcilable values of pluralism and secularism. Pluralism means respecting differences of religion, culture and values. Ideally, no one community can impose its cultural and religious values on other communities. Citizens are free to express their identity in the public

---

[6] Kevin Y.L. Tan and Li-Ann Thio, *Singapore: 50 constitutional moments that defined a nation* (Singapore: Marshall Cavendish, 2015), pp. 129–135.

[7] Kevin Y.L. Tan and Li-Ann Thio, *Singapore: 50 constitutional moments that defined a nation*, p. 133.

domain, celebrating diversity.[8] The Singapore government believes that each community is unique and separate from others, though in reality, it also aspires towards the assimilation of minority and immigrant communities with the Chinese majority into a united Singapore identity.[9] On the other hand, secularism means that there are restrictions imposed on communities preventing them from projecting their religious identities overtly in the public domain. Religious beliefs should be kept to the private domain. How secularism is understood differs from one country to another and there is also a very thin line separating religious and non-religious issues.

It is clear that in Singapore, one must not push a religious belief at the expense of other religious beliefs. The tension between pluralism and secularism is evident in the country. For example, some Malay women reckoned that in the spirit of pluralism, which celebrates their identity and freedom of religion, they should be allowed to don the headscarf (*tudung*) at their workplace. The state has a different view. In light of the state's secular principles, the *tudung* is not allowed for those working in frontline jobs and uniform groups such as nurses and police. In another example, the Ministry of Home Affairs (MHA) had imposed some controversial restrictions, including the use of musical instruments, during the Thaipusam festival in 2013. During this Hindu procession, devotees will perform a fourkilometre walk from the Sri Srinivasa Perumal temple at Serangoon Road to the Sri Thendayuthapani temple (Chettiars' temple) at Tank Road, carrying offerings and spikes attached to their bodies. The walk is accompanied with music and prayers.[10] To some, this is restricting their freedom of religious practice.

There has also been some requests made by the Hindu community to declare the Thaipusam a public holiday, as it was in the past.

---

[8] Bilveer Singh, *Politics and governance in Singapore: An introduction* (Singapore: McGraw Hill, 2012), p. 114.

[9] Michael Barr and Jevon Low, "Assimilation as multiracialism: The case of Singapore's Malays", *Asian Ethnicity* 6(3), pp. 161–182, 2005.

[10] "MHA sets out reasons for Thaipusam restrictions", *Today Online*, 14 February 2015. Retrieved on 30 November 2016 from http://www.todayonline.com/singapore/thaipusam-procession-poses-unique-challenges-keeping-law-and-order-mha

In Singapore, the government declares public holidays for the main religious and ethnic groups. The public holidays are allocated as follows: for the Chinese, two days of Chinese New Year holidays; Malays/Muslims, a day for Hari Raya Aidilfitri and a day for Hari Raya Aidiladha; Buddhists, one day for Vesak Day; Hindus, one day for Deepavali; and Christians/Catholics, a day for Good Friday and a day for Christmas Day. The Manpower Ministry, however, rejected the requests to make Thaipusam a public holiday because it will invite "competing claims".

Singapore's Brand of Multiculturalism

Singapore's experience in dealing with bloody ethnic clashes in the 1950s and 1960s coloured the government's official narrative on multiculturalism. On 21 July 1964, Singapore witnessed a bloody racial riot that would change the course of the country's nation building efforts. Popularly known as the *Maulid Nabi* riot, a group of Malays/Muslims and Chinese clashed during the Prophet Muhammad's birthday procession. Then Prime Minister Lee Kuan Yew claimed that leaders of Malaysia's ruling party, UMNO (United Malays National Organisation) instigated the Malays against the Chinese several days before the event. Tensions between the two communities were already brewing months before the riots, with UMNO-owned newspaper, *Utusan Melayu*, featuring articles accusing the Singapore PAP (People's Action Party) government of practising discrimination towards Singapore Malays.[11] The *Maulid Nabi* clashes saw 23 dead and 454 injured. That was the second major riot within a span of two

---

[11] *Utusan Melayu* was founded by Yusof Ishak in 1939. It is a Malay-rights newspaper. UMNO bought the newspaper, and Yusof resigned as its managing editor. Yusof later became the first local *Yang di-Pertuan Negara* (Head of State) of Singapore. Nine days before the riot, UMNO secretary general, Syed Jaafar Albar, spoke at a rally labelling the Singapore Malay/Muslim Members of Parliament "un-Islamic", "anti-Islam", and "traitors" to the Malay race. See Kuan Yew Lee, *The Singapore Story: Memoirs of Lee Kuan Yew* (Singapore: Singapore Press Holdings/Times Edition, 1998).

decades. In 1950, the country had to manage the Maria Hertogh riot, after a section of the Muslim community protested a court ruling that Maria — adopted and raised by Muslim parents — be returned to her biological parents who were Catholics. What angered the Muslims was that Maria was already married to a Muslim, and she had converted to Catholicism after returning to her real parents. The riot saw 18 people dead and several hundreds injured.

The politicisation of ethnicity was one of the reasons why Singapore was expelled from Malaysia in August 1965. On 9 August that year, Singapore gained independence after being part of Malaysia for less than two years.[12] The main disagreement that led to the separation was that the PAP government of Singapore called for a Malaysian Malaysia based on the principles of multiracialism and meritocracy, where all ethnic groups are free to express their identity and there is equality of opportunity for all races. On the flipside, UMNO politicians wanted to uphold the spirit of *ketuanan Melayu* or Malay supremacy. They wanted the Malays to retain their dominance in politics, but did not mind non-Malays spearheading the country's economy.

Since the 1964 riot, Singapore has not seen any form of ethnic tensions of that nature, except for a minor one in May 1969 that was also racially motivated. It took almost five decades later — in December 2013 — that the country faced a large-scale protest. Four hundred foreign workers from India demonstrated at Little India after seeing one of their countrymen being hit by a bus and died. The police Special Operations Command (SOC) and Gurkha Contingent, the two main units that handle mass protests and riots in the country, were called into action, and quickly quelled the disturbance. According to the Penal Code, an assembly of five or more persons can be deemed as unlawful if guilty of the following: such as using force against legislative or executive government or public servants exercising their duties; resisting the execution of law; or compelling someone, through the use of criminal force, to do something he is not

---

[12] Singapore obtained self-rule in 1959, and subsequently joined Malaysia in September 1963.

legally bound to do. The perpetrators can be charged for rioting if any members in the unlawful assembly use force.[13] The swiftness in the way the Singapore authorities managed the Little India riots shows that they are well-prepared when facing such circumstances, conveying a repeat of what happened in 1964 would not be tolerated.[14]

In its effort to prevent such riots from happening in Singapore, the government adopted a strong-hand approach when managing ethnic relations. Its nation building efforts emphasised on two essential values: meritocracy and multiculturalism. Both underscore Singapore's race-blind approach where citizens are rewarded on the basis of their hard work. The government upholds these traits to distinguish itself from its neighbour Malaysia, which is muddled with race-based politics and affirmative action which privileges the Malays and *Bumiputeras* (sons of the soil). In Singapore, the government feels the Malays should compete fairly with the other ethnic communities in education and work. However, in practice, Singapore has never been a pure meritocratic society. The government has always adopted an 'abridged meritocracy' because ethnic categories still matter. Elements of ethnic-based politics and affirmative action are still present in the country, though in a lesser degree compared to Malaysia. Abridged meritocracy is not necessarily negative because it has paved the way for minority communities to integrate into the system. As I will discuss shortly, the Group Representation Constituency (GRC) and recent amendments to the Elected President (EP) in 2016 ensure that minority representation is safeguarded. These two schemes not only manifest abridged meritocracy, they also entrench the state's CMIO multiculturalism (each alphabet representing the ethnic groups Chinese, Malays, Indians, and Others).

---

[13] Attorney-General's Chambers, *Singapore statutes online, chapter VIII, offences relating to unlawful assembly* (Singapore: The Author). Retrieved on 28 December 2016 from http://statutes.agc.gov.sg/aol/search/display/view.w3p;ident=eb3d032c-5e81-4348-87ff-f88cf1e51074;page=0;query=DocId%3A%22025e7646-947b-462c-b557-60aa55dc7b42%22%20Status%3Ainforce%20Depth%3A0;rec=0

[14] Little India is a small town in Singapore that has historically been considered an Indian enclave.

The CMIO model cannot be attributed to the PAP government alone. At the risk of generalising, policies undertaken by the colonial government, Singapore's experience in Malaysia, and immigration (intensified by globalisation) contribute to Singapore's multiculturalism. Most Western colonial powers in Asia and Africa adopted the divide-and-rule strategy which capitalised on existing ethnic cleavages to leverage control of colonised populations. By playing out ethnic and religious tensions, though not necessarily in violent manner all the time, colonial officials planted distrust among the different groups to weaken them internally. Since they are internally disunited, the locals could not mount a challenge against their colonial masters.[15] It was also the colonial way of giving special treatments to certain groups but not to others. These privileges include access to education, positions in the civil service, and appointments in legislative assemblies.

In the same vein, colonial governments also adopted a hierarchy of ethnicity in the states they govern, where some ethnic groups were regarded as industrious and hardworking while others were considered lazy. Tracing the biased attitudes of colonial officials towards the natives in the Malay world, which includes today's Brunei, Indonesia, Malaysia, and Singapore, Syed Hussein Alatas wrote an influential book *The Myth of the Lazy Native* to discuss how different ethnic groups' acceptance towards colonial capitalism determines the colonials' views towards industriousness.[16] The British's capitalistic ventures in the mid-19th century opened the doors for foreign labour from south China, India, Malaya and Indonesia, which led to the influx of immigrants. So open was the British policy towards immigration, which helped expand the tin mining and rubber plantations industry that the Chinese community became the majority in Singapore. The Malay's lack of response towards colonial capitalism earned them the title 'lazy Malays'.

---

[15] Baogang He and Will Kymlicka, "Introduction", in Will Kymlicka and Baogang He (eds.), *Multiculturalism in Asia* (pp. 1–21) (Oxford, England: Oxford University Press, 2005), p. 7.

[16] Syed Hussein Alatas, *The myth of the lazy native* (London, England: F Cass, 1977).

In line with their ethnocentric views of the natives, the colonials treated ethnic groups as homogeneous, unchanging, and static. They were also responsible for categorising the different ethnic groups through census making. Various dialect and racial groups were subsumed into umbrella ethnic categories such as 'Chinese', 'Indians' and 'Malays'. Over time, Chinese dialect groups such as Hokkiens, Teochews and Hakkas were all absorbed into one category, the Chinese. Similarly, the Ambonese, Banjaris, Boyanese, Bugis and Javanese were all categorised as Malays.

The crystallisation of CMIO continued even after Singapore became part of Malaysia. Though there were nationalist and communist-based parties which struggled on the basis of class and affiliation to the land (*tanah air*), Malaya (before 1963) saw the birth of ethnic-based political parties. In the Peninsular, there are parties for the Malays (UMNO); for the Indians (Malaysian Indian Congress, MIC); and for the Chinese (Malaysian Chinese Association, MCA). The multicultural ideology proposed by PAP leaders is also a reaction to the political situation in Malaysia, which promotes Malay dominance and special privileges for the indigenous peoples. Disagreeing fundamentally with Malaysian leaders, the PAP campaigned for a Malaysian Malaysia, premised on equality and meritocracy. It continued to uphold these principles when Singapore gained independence in 1965. Occasionally, both leaders across the Causeway make remarks about each other's ideology. Singapore leaders pride in achieving equality in their country with meritocracy, while Malaysian leaders claim they have succeeded in developing a progressive Malay community. Prime Minister Mahathir Mohamed (1981–2003) had always claimed that the Malays in Singapore are marginalised and weak, while Singapore leaders countered by saying that they managed the minority Malays better.

The contribution of Singapore's pioneers was key in sustaining multiculturalism. Much has been written about Lee Kuan Yew and PAP leaders on their belief in multiculturalism, which was later incorporated into Singapore's national pledge. The pledge contains the phrase "regardless of race, language or religion". Yet, for multiculturalism to succeed, it requires the support of minority leaders.

Singapore's first President, Yusof Ishak, was one Malay community leader to support multiculturalism.[17] As the President, he was a strong advocate of multiculturalism, and relentlessly emphasised the importance of building a strong united society. It would have been easier if Yusof had supported Malaysia's position on race relations. Several Malay leaders, such as Yusof and members of the literati, including teachers and laureates, stayed in Singapore despite invitation by the Malaysian UMNO leaders to cross over to take up citizenship in Malaysia and form part of the majority. Similarly, in the period of uncertainty, Chinese and Indians in Singapore stayed, even though they had the choice of crossing to neighbouring countries, including going back to India and China. Their decision to stay makes up a multiracial Singapore.

Singapore's Multicultural Ideology on Political and Social Fronts

The way national leaders understand multiculturalism and meritocracy has a profound impact on society. The first four presidents of the Republic (between 1965 and 1993) showcase the core tenets of CMIO multiculturalism. There was an unspoken rotation of the presidency among the four ethnic groups: the first President is a Malay, Yusof Ishak; and he is followed by a Eurasian, Dr. Benjamin Sheares; an Indian, Devan Nair; and a Chinese, Dr. Wee Kim Wee. Since 1993, the government amended the constitution and the country's President is directly elected by the people. The amendment also means that the President has custodial powers to veto how the monetary reserves are used by the government of the day. Since the President is elected by Singaporeans, selection of the head of state on the basis of his ethnicity ceased. In 1993, Ong Teng Cheong was the first President to be directly elected by the people, and he is a Chinese. In 1999, S.R. Nathan, an Indian, was the second President after the

---

[17] Norshahril Saat, *Yusof Ishak: Singapore's first President* (Singapore: Institute of Southeast Asian Studies, 2015).

constitutional amendment. He assumed the position without political contest, and was elected unopposed. In 2011, former Deputy Prime Minister, Dr. Tony Tan, a Chinese was the third elected President in a four-way contest. Had the system remained as president by appointment and not by election, the President after S.R. Nathan should be a Malay or Eurasian. In fact, during the 2011 election, all four candidates were Chinese.

In 2016, Prime Minister Lee Hsien Loong suggested that the EP scheme be revised again to ensure that minority candidates have an equal chance to become president. Prime Minister Lee openly said his desire to see a Malay president. A committee was set up to hear submissions from the public on how best the system could be tweaked. Responses have been mixed because some wanted a president to be elected based on merit. On the other hand, some hoped that minorities be given a chance to lead the country. Prime Minister Lee's rationale for the change was that minority communities must believe that they have a place in Singapore. In the same year, the constitution was amended and the EP scheme was altered. The 2016 amendment introduced a controversial hiatus-triggered model which means that if there are no candidates from an ethnic community elected for five terms in a row, the following elections will be reserved for that particular community. The change meant that 2017 presidential elections was reserved for the Malays because no one from the community was elected since Dr. Wee Kim Wee. Responding to criticisms that such changes only entrenche race-based politics in the country, the government pointed out that the qualifying criteria is not lowered. The candidate has to have experience holding important positions in the public sector, such as being Permanent Secretary, Minister, or a Speaker of Parliament. Candidates from the private sector are welcome to contest, but he must have held the most senior executive role in a company with S$500 million of shareholders' equity. Some members of the Malay community have expressed their unhappiness about this amendment. They regard this as a form of tokenism to the community and believe the Malays can one day be elected President in an open contest with other ethnic groups.

Multiculturalism directly conditions the distribution of parliamentary seats and hence, political power. Singapore adopts a parliamentary democracy model from the British but in 1988, it introduced the GRC. It means that rather than having one candidate contesting in a single ward, the scheme introduces 'team MPs' for a particular constituency. As a result of this change, in 1988, 39 single-member constituencies were placed under 13 GRCs.[18] The rationale of the GRC was to ensure that minority candidates could be elected into Parliament. In each GRC, there has to be at least one minority candidate. The remaining seats in the GRC belong to the Chinese.

The scheme has been criticised on several reasons. First, it weakens the chance of the opposition to win a GRC.[19] Since its introduction, no opposition party has ever won a GRC. It was only in 2011 and 2015 that the Workers' Party (WP) won at the Aljunied GRC, even though the opposition came close to winning a GRC a number of times as in the Bedok, Eunos and Cheng San GRCs prior to 2011. The GRC also demonstrates that Members of Parliament (MPs) are not voted because of merit but by their ethnicity. Some have accused new MPs of being sheltered by Ministers, who helm a GRC each. The scheme makes voters think again for voting the opposition, because they may lose a Minister if the PAP does not win the constituency. PAP's defeat at Aljunied in 2011 meant the loss of Minister for Foreign Affairs George Yeo and Lim Hwee Hua, Minister in the Prime Minister's Office.

Although the GRC scheme is meant to ensure minority representation, critics argue that they are unable to choose their own leaders. They posit that the minority MPs are handpicked by the government and do not articulate community interests in Parliament. In 1990, members of the Association of Muslim Professionals (AMP) called for

---

[18] Norshahril Saat, "Singapore beyond ethnicity: Rethinking the Group Representative Constituency Scheme", *The Round Table: The Commonwealth Journal of International Affairs*, 105(2), pp. 195–203, 2016; and Hussin Mutalib, *Parties and politics: A study of opposition parties and the PAP in Singapore* (Singapore: Eastern University Press, 2003).

[19] Hussin Mutalib, *Parties and politics: A study of opposition parties and the PAP in Singapore*.

a collective leadership for the Malay community, so that the Malay leadership does not only include PAP Malay MPs.[20]

Apart from the political front, multiculturalism has also shaped Singapore's education policy. Schools require students to take vernacular languages (now known as mother tongue and second languages in the past) based on the ethnic group they belong to. For example, Malay students are required to take *Bahasa Melayu*, while the Chinese students have to study Mandarin, and Indians, Tamil. Most schools do not offer dialects — such as Hokkien, Cantonese, Malayalee, Gujerati, Urdu, and Punjabi — even though since 1990, there are the Non-Tamil Indian Languages (NTILs) for students taking Punjabi, Urdu, Gujerati, Bengali and Hindi, usually in weekend classes but some are conducted in mainstream schools during curriculum time. Students are required to take these mother tongue languages, and failing which, they may not be allowed to progress to the next level of their studies, or they do not qualify to take certain subjects. Although mother tongue languages are made compulsory, English is the medium of instruction for all subjects. While most students are able to cope with the government's bilingual policy, increasingly the standards for mother tongue subjects have dropped. The government, MPs and members of the civil society have worked together to improve the standards of mother tongue languages in the country. In 1979, then Prime Minister Lee Kuan Yew launched the 'Speak Mandarin' campaign to improve Singaporeans' proficiency of the language and communication among Chinese Singaporeans. The Malay community too organises its annual *Bulan Bahasa* (Malay language month) for similar reasons.

The ideology of multiculturalism is also extended to the realm of social services. The CMIO model defines what Singaporeans identify as community self-help groups. The basis for such groups is that each community supports its own institutions to help alleviate problems

---

[20] Hussin Mutalib, *Singapore Malays: Being ethnic minority and Muslim in a global city-state* (Oxfordshire, England: Routledge, 2012); and Lily Rahim, *The Singapore dilemma: The political and educational marginality of the Malay community* (Kuala Lumpur, Malaysia: Oxford University Press, 1998).

associated with the community. For instance, in the 1980s, Malay leaders organised a convention discussing the community's under-achievement in education. In 1982, the Malays then got their act together to form Mendaki (Council for the Development of Singapore Malay/Muslim Community). The organisation is responsible for organising tuition classes for Malays to improve their academic achievements in the field of Mathematics and Science. The organisation is also responsible for providing financial aid to poor students in order for them to improve their education. Mendaki has also evolved to conduct skills upgrading training for workers.

The Indian and Chinese communities have similar organisations equivalent to that of Mendaki. SINDA (Singapore Indian Development Association) was formed by the Indian community whereas CDAC (Chinese Development Assistance Council) was created by the Chinese. These self-help groups have been criticised for several reasons, chief of which is that they help promote primordial ethnic sentiments. Furthermore, the ability of the Chinese to mobilise resources better than the Indians and the Malays have also worsened these ethnic sentiments.[21] The other criticism levelled at the ethnic self-help groups is that it is an inefficient way of helping students in their studies. Scholars who adopt a structuralist perspective would argue that educational achievement is linked to class. The upper- and middle-class families can afford tuition and better assessment books for their children, hence, they have an earlier start compared to those from the lower class. Without a doubt, Mendaki and the other self-help groups have focused on helping members from the lower class. They help in providing tuition for them and also interest-free loans for Malays who cannot afford their tertiary education. Mendaki and the other self-help groups have evolved in a way that although they remain stuck in ethnicised ideology, they also factor class dynamics in their assistance programmes.

---

[21] Lily Rahim, "The paradox of ethnic-based self-help groups", in Derek da Cunha (ed.), *Debating Singapore: Reflective essays* (pp. 46–50) (Singapore: Institue of Southeast Asian Studies, 1996).

Generally, multiculturalism in Singapore today is not only state-led but also led by civil society as well. One great embodiment of multiculturalism was the formation of the Inter-Religious Organisation (IRO). Formed in 1949, the IRO's objective has been to foster peace and religious harmony in Singapore. It conducts many interfaith dialogues and interfaith prayers. Sitting on the IRO council are key leaders of the various religious groups in the country, representing Islam, Buddhism, Sikhism, Taoism, Judaism, Hinduism, Christianity and others. The IRO is an example of ground-up efforts, and functions like an NGO (non-governmental organisation) in fostering multiculturalism in Singapore. There are many other interfaith organisations in Singapore that sprung up after the 9/11 attacks, and many are religious-centric rather than cultural-centric. For example, the Islamic Religious Council of Singapore (MUIS) hosted the Harmony Centre with the same aim of fostering peace and harmony among different religious groups in Singapore. The principal aim was to avoid misunderstandings others may have towards Islam. There are also efforts undertaken by Singapore mosques, which encourage people of other faiths to visit them. Every year, some mosques in Singapore would invite non-Muslims to attend the Ramadhan *iftars* (breaking of fast during Ramadhan). This is to encourage more non-Muslims to join and understand the Muslim rituals together. Many of the Christian followers have also participated in interfaith missions, and one of them is reverent Yap Kim Hao, who has been actively promoting dialogue among different religious groups.

Multiculturalism leading to culturalism

While the main objective of multiculturalism is to instil trust among different ethnic groups, it has also promoted the unintended effects of ethnocentrism and prejudice. Often, assessments of criminals, performance in schools, and success in career are described in ethnic terms. In the 1970s, the Malay community was associated with high numbers of drug abuses. When casinos were introduced in Singapore in the 2000s, problems associated with gambling were associated with the Chinese community. After 9/11 and the threat of *Jemaah Islamiyah*'s (JI) terrorism in the 2000s, the government placed the spotlight on the Malay/Muslim community, even though the problem was not only a religious one but also socioeconomic and geopolitical in nature. The community has also come forward to own the problems by setting up institutions such as the Religious Rehabilitation Group (RRG) in order to provide counselling to JI detainees and prevent radicalisation.

The racialisation of problems also coloured how society judges their leaders. Can an Indian or a Malay become the Prime Minister of the country? So far, Indians have been appointed into important positions of the Cabinet, as ministers for Foreign Affairs, Finance, Law, and Trade and Industry. The Indian community has also seen three becoming Deputy Prime Ministers from the community: Tharman Shanmugaratnam (2011 to present), S. Jayakumar (2004 to 2009), and S. Rajaratnam (1980 to 1985). Malay politicians have held various portfolios of Environment and Water Resources as well as Community Development, Youth and Sports. Dr. Yaacob Ibrahim was probably the first Malay to become the Minister for Information, Communication and the Arts. Based on a survey conducted on 2,000 Singaporeans by *Channel NewsAsia* (CNA) and Institute of Policy Studies (IPS), ethnicity remains crucial in the selection of leaders by the community. For example, 98% of Chinese surveyed can accept a Chinese to be Prime Minister but less than 60% can accept a Malay or an Indian. Only 59% of Chinese respondents can accept a Malay president and 68% an Indian president. Malay and Indian respondents showed higher figures in accepting other ethnicity as their leaders. The respondents shared that they heard racist comments from the friends, colleagues, family members and online contacts.[22]

While it is important for Singapore to address the ethnic problem at the leadership level, the problem is to prevent racism from trickling down at the societal level. The government takes discriminatory practices against minorities at the workplace very seriously, and has urged employers not to discriminate workers based on their race. There have

---

[22] "Racism still a problem for some Singaporeans, CNA-IPS survey finds", *Channel NewsAsia*, 18 August 2016. Retrieved on 24 November 2016 from http://www.channelnewsasia.com/news/singapore/racism-still-a-problem/3043764.html

been complaints that some work advertisements have preferred workers who can speak Mandarin, in which most Malays or Indians cannot. While there have been improvements in this aspect, more needs to be done before racism is eradicated.

Conclusion: Multiculturalism in the Age of New Media

In age of new media, opinions expressed by individuals are no longer deemed personal but public. Personal comments could be misconstrued leading to uneasy social tensions. Defining multiculturalism is even more complex as the CMIO categorisation has expanded to include foreign nationals. Some individuals from within the CMIO communities are also challenging what it means to be Chinese, Malays, and Indians. To conclude, the following paragraphs will point out three incidences which showcase how Singapore's multicultural fabric is being challenged. Two of the cases discussed involve squabbles between foreign nationals and locals. The cases here demonstrate how conflicts can harm Singapore's multicultural fabric in the future if not carefully managed by the authorities and civil society.

First, in 2011, Singaporeans were shocked to learn about what is called the "Curry dispute". An article in *Today* (Mediacorp-owned free newspaper) reported that a newly arrived family from China complained that their Indian (local) neighbours cooked curry and the smell from the cooking caused displeasure to them. The Indian family were tolerant of the complaints and went to the extent of closing their windows every time they cook curry but this did not satisfy the Chinese family. The matter was then raised to the Community Mediation Centre (CMC), which handles disputes among neighbours. It was reported that the CMC urged the Indian family to only cook curry when their Chinese neighbours were not at home. This angered many Singaporeans who felt that the mediator was biased against the Indian family. It was later clarified that the mediator was neutral in handling the situation, and it was the two families which cordially reached the agreement. Reacting to this incident, writer

Florence Leow started a 'Cook and Share a Pot of Curry' Facebook page to encourage greater appreciation of the Indian cuisine.

Second, Singaporeans were appalled by the behaviour of eighteen-year-old teenager, Amos Yee, who had uploaded videos belittling Christians and Muslims. Yee was arrested and this drew international flak. The Western media felt that Yee was mainly exercising freedom of expression. Though Yee may be a rare case, the incident indicates the kind of society that Singapore will see 10 years down the road. The young are willing to trade multiculturalism in the name of liberty, and we see glimpses of this through comments made in social media.

Third, in March 2016, former editor of *The Real Singapore* (TRS) website, Ai Tagaki, was sentenced to jail for inciting hatred towards foreign nationals. She authored and falsified an article which pitted the Filipino community in Singapore against Indians. Tagaki edited an article claiming that a Filipino family called the police to stop the participants of the Thaipusam procession from playing the drums. The playing of music and drums is common in the procession, and has been practised in Singapore for decades. The false article gave the wrong impression that foreigners were against a cultural practice by Indian Singaporeans. Police investigations showed how Tagaki made up the story and it was not true. The police and courts' intervention prevented what could be harmful in society. It could have created unnecessary tensions between the local Indian communities with the Filipino nationals.

There have been criticisms that the way Singapore government manages freedom of expression is against the values of human rights and individual liberties. The more fundamental question is whether Singapore society is ready to be given a free hand to manage ethnic issues? The government's intervention is necessary in the event where society cannot manage differences amicably. Singaporeans have matured through government intervention, but whether they have developed enough savvy in handling ethnic issues remains wanting. While there have been many initiatives undertaken by government agencies and civil society which foster harmony among different reli-gious groups, the situation today is certainly far from ideal, especially in the context of rising religiosity and influx of foreign nationals.

Singapore's multicultural ideology will continue to shape the official narrative of the state. While it has many unintended consequences, especially the promotion of culturalism when discussing problems, and creation of prejudices, it also has its merits of maintaining peace and stability of the country. Almost all the initiatives relating to multiculturalism are state-led: the government's strong intervention in ensuring racial slurs do not go out of hand. Civil society groups have also participated effectively in ensuring the success of multiculturalism. A strong combination of state's heavy-handedness on racial issues to the development of appreciation by the masses, helps maintain religious harmony in Singapore. In a globalised world, and in the age of social media, Singaporeans will be confronted with greater challenges that will question multiculturalism. It is hoped that more and more Singaporeans will not only tolerate diversity and other cultures, but will be appreciative of differences.

The bigger challenge is to develop a good sense of appreciation towards diversity. As it is, Singaporeans feel that multiculturalism is superimposed by the government, civil society or the elders in their respective communities which means that it remains an elite-level discourse. More efforts should be invested in building the capacity for ground-level or day-to-day multicultural spirit, be that at the workplace or online. As such efforts grow, Singaporeans can truly call their country a race-blind one in the future.

Multiracialism is an asset to Singapore's nation building efforts. Ideally, a country should adopt race-blind approach when managing its people, but race-based politics is not easy to deal with. Some would even think it is human nature, but has to be controlled. Singapore leaders' vision of multicultural thinking is indeed a forward-thinking one. In the last years starting from 2011, many developed countries in Europe and the United States are becoming more critical towards immigrants. In 2016, Republican Donald Trump was elected as the U.S. President campaigning along rightist principles. Singapore has managed ethnic issues well through its brand of heavy and soft multiculturalism. As Singapore approaches the ideal of becoming race-blind, it has to continue with its policy of managing differences inter and intra ethnic groups.

Chapter 4

Political Innovations and Stabilisers as Strategic Assets in Singapore

Bilveer Singh

Introduction

Upon gaining political independence and sovereignty on 9 August 1965, Singapore adopted a Westminster parliamentary system. Despite being part of Malaysia from September 1963 to August 1965, elements of the colonial parliamentary system were already in place since 1955 following the adoption of the Rendel Commission Report in 1954. The Constitution came into effect on 8 February 1955.[1] With minor modifications in 1958, 1963 and 1965, the essence of the British political inheritance was in place when independence was thrust on Singapore in August 1965. This was a system where the executive was drawn from the legislative. The rules of the engagement were very clear with Members of Parliament (MPs) elected by popular vote and the political party with the largest number of MPs invited by the Head of State, in this case, the President, to form the government. The Prime Minister then selected his ministers from the elected MPs to form the Cabinet.

---

[1] State of Singapore, Government Gazette, Extraordinary, Singapore, G.N. 309, p. 153, 1955, February 5.

Singapore has a unicameral house and has held regular elections since independence. However, since 1965, the inherited political system has been systematically altered and the Westminster system, in essence, modified. All these changes were made by a political party in power since the 1959 general elections and whose dominance of the system has been total. Against this backdrop, this study aims to explain the reasons behind the continuous changes to the political system and what this means for the future of the one-party dominant system in Singapore, currently seen as one of the most successful states in the world, especially economically.

The Rise of Singapore as a One-Party Dominant State

The term 'dominant' was popularised by Maurice Duverger in 1951, analysing the dynamics of the emergence of a dominant political party in multiparty democracies.[2] The one-party dominant state is different from a one-party state found in communist countries such as China. The end of the Cold War and what Samuel Huntington described as the 'Third Wave of Democratization' did not preclude the rise of a one-party dominant state.[3] This political system seems to have endured in many countries and even gained legitimacy, with the ability of such states to score high on various aspects of governance, including providing goods related to national security, social stability and economic development. In this regard, Singapore, where the ruling party, the People's Action Party (PAP), though operating in a multiparty system, has been continuously in power since 1959, has particularly stood out. Following the 2015 general elections, the PAP was again returned to office with even a stronger mandate than what it gained in the 2011 elections (see Table 4.1).

---

[2] Maurice Duverger, *Les partis politiques* (Paris, France: Armand Colin, 1951).
[3] Samuel P. Huntington, *The third wave: Democratization in the late 20th century* (Oklahoma: University of Oklahoma Press, 1991).

Table 4.1. Singapore general election results, 1959–2015

Year	Seats	% Votes
1959	43	53.4
1963	37	46.4
1968	58	84.4
1972	65	69.0
1976	69	72.4
1980	75	75.5
1984	77	62.9
1988	80	61.7
1991	77	59.3
1997	81	63.5
2001	82	75.3
2006	82	66.6
2011	81	60.1
2015	83	69.9

Source: Author.

Singapore fits the characteristics of a one-party dominant state. Giovanni Sartori describes a one-party dominant system as one where the same party wins an absolute majority in at least three consecutive elections.[4] T.J. Pempel points out that despite free electoral competition, relatively open information systems, respect for civil liberties, and the right of free political association in a number of states across Asia and Africa, a single party has managed to govern alone or as the primary and on-going partner in coalitions, without interruption, for substantial periods of time.[5] For Pempel, a political party is considered 'dominant' if it is dominant in numbers, securing at least a plurality

---

[4] Giovanni Sartori, *Parties and party systems: A framework for analysis vol. 1* (New York: Cambridge University Press, 1976).
[5] T.J. Pempel (ed.), *Uncommon democracies* (Cornell, NY: Cornell University Press, 1990), p. 1.

of votes and seats but this counts if the party is electorally dominant for an uninterrupted and prolonged period; it must enjoy a dominant bargaining position, always setting the tone when it comes to government formation; and it must be dominant governmentally and determine the public policy agenda.[6]

Many factors help to explain the endurance of the one-party dominant system and state. First, there is the role of history.[7] In systems that have a one-party dominant system, the states have experienced colonialism, civil war or repression under a civilian or military regime. Many of the ruling parties in such states emerged as nationalist movements that mobilised the citizens to fight for independence, for new political arrangements and even championed the democratisation movements. These parties become dominant as they are seen to be progenitors of nationalism and the modern state, and often succeed in creating a new state and system in its image.

Second, most of the dominant parties emerged as 'national' or 'nationalist' parties, transcending national racial, religious, linguistic and economic fault lines. This is also in part due to the fact that these parties are also broad-based multi-ethnic, multi-religious and multi-linguistic parties and representative of the national economic strata rather than a particular class. Most of the newer parties, however, partly due to the competitive nature of democracy, tend to be associated with a particular agenda and often tend to have a more particularistic following or support base. While the older nationalist or national parties tend to transcend multiple cleavages, its success in doing so also helps to ensure its staying power in politics.

Third, as argued by Duverger and Arend Lijphart, the nature of electoral system and institutional arrangement can also play a part in

---

[6] See Clemens Spiess, *Democracy and party system in developing countries: A comparative study of India and South Africa* (Routledge Advances in South Asian Studies), 1st Edition (London, England: Routledge, 2009), p. 12.

[7] Samuel P. Huntington, *The third wave: Democratization in the late 20th century*; Hermann Giliomee and Charles Simkins (eds.), *The awkward embrace: One party dominance and democracy* (Cape Town, South Africa: Tafelberg, 1999).

instituting the endurance of a one-party dominant state. While proportional representation systems allow small parties to win seats in parliament, thereby causing party system fragmentation, the majoritarian first-past-the-post system tends to reinforce political dominance.

Fourth, a state's political culture can also affect and influence that emergence of a dominant party system. When a nation's political institutions like the dominant political party is fused with national cultural norms and where the party is seen as the personification of the state and its people, it can assist in the strengthening of a one-party dominant state.

Fifth, no political party can remain in power unless it proves itself and demonstrates performance legitimacy. A failed party is unlikely to survive and hence, governmental performance is an important factor in explaining the longevity of political parties and their dominance. While people may support a dominant political party due to emotional ties, backing for its ideology and historical role, for many, it is because it is a performing party. In short, rationality and meritocracy are equally important factors in explaining the endurance of the one-party dominant state.

At the same time, the ability of a dominant party to avoid mistakes that can lead to its collapse, can also embed and entrench a party's political longevity in a state. While the rise and sustenance of a one-party dominant system has been a fact, it is also true that many of these dominant parties have eventually been defeated at the ballot boxes. Why do one-party dominant systems collapse? First, it is mainly due to the failure to perform economically, as was the case in Indonesia. Related to this is often the case of abuse of power after years of unchecked dominance in the system. Second, is the ability of the opposition to gain legitimacy as a contender for government, often made possible by the manifold failure of the dominant party in power and which often lead to prolonged problems and crises. Due to various failures and shortcomings, the dominant party is unable to maintain its power base. It can also result from a maturity of the political society that believes in checks and balances, all the more, if credible alternatives are available. There is also the image aspect with the society as a whole wanting to demonstrate that it is in step with global democratisation phenomenon, especially when the one-party dominant system is not working.

Political Innovations in a Small One-Party Dominant State

As a former British colony, Singapore adopted a political system of its former colonial master. The ceremonial head of state is the President and the Prime Minister is the head of government. Singapore has a unicameral house and since independence in 1965, it has held regular elections to elect MPs. Although the Singapore government is modeled after that of the British, it has introduced several innovations to the system of government leading many to question whether the system of government in place in Singapore can still be referred to as a Westminster parliamentary system. The key innovations include the Non-Constituency Member of Parliament (NCMP), Nominated Member of Parliament (NMP), Group Representation Constituencies (GRCs) and the Elected President (EP). The objective of these innovations is to inject a high degree of stability with the hope of bequeathing a reformed political system that is not only relevant to Singapore but also an asset to future generations of Singaporeans.

The NCMP system

The NCMP scheme was introduced in 1984 to ensure the inclusion of the Opposition in parliament. It was to provide opposition members who had lost in the general elections but for being the best losers, they could have a seat in Parliament. Initially, up to three of the 'best losers' in a general election could be inducted into Parliament as NCMPs with limited voting powers. The government's rationale for the introduction of the scheme was to inject greater debates in Parliament, fueled by the tacit acknowledgement of the impotency of the Opposition to win in general elections. The scheme was meant to provide a 'backdoor entry' for the Opposition into Parliament. This system was at first received negatively by opposition leaders who viewed the arrangement as an insult to the Opposition. However, the opposition leaders finally accepted the offer after recognising the benefit of being in Parliament. NCMPs, while having limited voting powers, are given the opportunity to raise questions in Parliament even though they cannot vote on money bills or on a vote of no confidence in the government.

Given that the PAP had controlled almost all seats in Parliament since 1965 and that the NCMPs have only limited voting rights, the NCMPs' role has been limited merely to being a 'voice' in parliamentary debate. Neither being able to influence PAP MPs nor having the ability to tip the balance of the arguments, the NCMP has effectively little impact on the voting patterns in Parliament. This effectively made the NCMP scheme as part of the PAP's pacification of the electorate. The effective message sent by the PAP through this scheme was that if the electorate wanted an opposition in Parliament, the PAP was willing to provide it. There was no need for the electorate to vote for the Opposition and against the PAP.

This innovation to the parliamentary system was arguably done by the PAP to accommodate the need for a non-threatening Opposition in parliament. First, shocked and later, coming to terms with the electorate's choice in the 1981 by-election and the 1984 general elections which saw the PAP's complete dominance of Parliament broken, the PAP was alleged to have introduced the scheme for two purposes. First, since it interpreted the actions of the electorate as a vote of disgruntlement rather than disapproval of the PAP, this scheme would pacify the electorate's desire for alternative voices in Parliament. Second, by admitting NCMPs into Parliament with limited voting rights, the PAP was implicitly portraying the Opposition as an impotent force, and in need of the good graces of the PAP. By satisfying the demands of the electorate while holding firm grip over Parliament, the PAP was able to retain its hegemony of the government and politics of Singapore.

The NCMP scheme was clearly a reformation of the original Westminster parliamentary system. Given that in some cases of Westminster parliamentary systems whereby some MPs are appointed rather than elected, the Singapore case is different as the

NCMPs, as originally conceived, have only limited voting rights and the rationale of their inclusion is certainly in need of further questioning. Rather than serving as an expansion to the plurality of views in Parliament, the NCMP scheme has been viewed as an attempt by the PAP to effectively neutralise any potential threat of opposition members being elected into parliament as full-fledged members.

Reflecting on the NCMP some 25 years later, Prime Minister Lee Hsien Loong noted that following the introduction of the scheme, the new team ministers and MPs concluded that "it was good for the government and good for the Singapore system that we have opposition in Parliament. The opposition members could express opposing views, could question and criticise the government, and could make Ministers justify their actions. The opposition provided Mr. Lee [Kuan Yew] and his team a 'foil' or backdrop against which they could set their ideas more clearly in contrast to what was being presented on the other side."[8] As opposition were seen as a good thing, whatever was the outcome in a general elections, there would at least be a certain minimum number of opposition in Parliament, be it on their own merit or through the NCMP scheme. The government also believed that the best losers had the right to be in Parliament compared to the proportional representation system as "the voters in the constituency which you contested have to have a sufficiently high regard to give you one of the highest votes among the losing candidates."[9] According to Prime Minister Lee, "you have got people who are really personally voting for you. I think that gives you legitimacy ...."[10] It also had the role of injecting greater political plurality in Parliament especially in a one-party dominant state.

---

[8] Zakir Hussain, "Changes to political system to prepare Singapore for long term: PM Lee Hsien Loong", *The Straits Times*, 28 January 2016.

[9] Zakir Hussain, "Changes to political system to prepare Singapore for long term: PM Lee Hsien Loong".

[10] Zakir Hussain, "Changes to political system to prepare Singapore for long term: PM Lee Hsien Loong".

The NMP system

The NMP scheme was introduced in 1991 during Goh Chok Tong's tenure as Singapore's Prime Minister. It refers to an MP who is appointed to Parliament by the President. Outstanding members of the public could be nominated to be non-partisan MP with limited voting powers. NMPs were to provide feedback, generate debates against MPs and contribute their individual talents and expertise in Parliament. The scheme was part of Goh's desire to develop a more consultative form of governance. Realising that there may be talented individuals in society who may shun public office due to the consequences of political life and given Singapore's limited talent pool, the scheme would allow such individuals to serve a two-year term in Parliament. Without the need to be a member of any political party and gain direct induction into Parliament without contesting in elections, it was hoped that more talented individuals would be willing to step forth and serve as NMPs. The first two NMPs were appointed in November 1990 and since 1997, the maximum number of NMPs has been increased from six to nine.

The introduction of this political innovation was taken in positive light as it allowed for the increase in the diversity of opinion in Parliament. However, since NMPs does not represent any political constituency, they too like NCMPs, have limited voting rights. Since its induction in the early 1990s, some NMPs, though not directly challenging the PAP hegemony in Parliament, have by their own right proved their worth by pushing for certain bills regarding social welfare issues to be passed in Parliament. For instance, in May 1994, NMP Walter Woon initiated a private member bill on the Maintenance of Parents Act that was passed in November 1995.

The GRC system

The GRC scheme was first introduced in 1988 and further refined in 1991, 1997, 2011 and 2016. It was to ensure a minimum number of minority race MPs in Parliament. It was also to enhance administration based on economies of scale (Ganesan, 1998, p. 230). The GRCs, which initially consisted of three-member groups, were expanded to four- and five-member groups, and later, to a maximum of six-member groups. In the formation of GRCs, it was also stipulated that at least one member of the groups must be a minority candidate, which means that one of the candidates must be of either Malay, Indian or Eurasian descent. This potential candidate is required to submit an application to the Elections Department to obtain a certification that confirms the applicant's ethnic minority status.

The rationale of such a policy by the PAP was to ensure sufficient ethnic minority representation in Parliament. Singapore's rigid housing quota policies have resulted in ethnic minorities losing their dominant enclaves, with Singapore emerging as one big Chinese enclave. Given the current demography of total Chinese electoral majorities in the electoral system, the PAP government was fearful that representatives of ethnic minorities may not be able to be voted in and hence, be accused of not taking the views of the ethnic minorities into consideration. While the action of enshrining minority representation is consistent with the PAP's pro-multi-ethnic governance, the Opposition has raised its objections against the GRCs. The GRC system is accused of favouring large political parties who have the necessary political machinery and funds to finance an enlarged constituency. Opposition parties, which were already challenged by their limited talent, manpower and funds, found it difficult to set up a team to contest for a GRC. Even when they did contest in one, the Opposition was fearful of losing its electoral deposit, which in the 2011 general elections stood at S$13,000 per candidate. A forfeit of their electoral deposit would certainly create a large dent in any opposition party's funds. Goh admitted that GRCs did favour large political parties, especially the PAP.[11]

It is common for PAP GRC teams to be anchored by a senior politician with the rest of the team being relatively new or weaker 'faces'. This often is perceived as the new PAP candidates 'riding on the tailcoat' of their much senior colleagues, even though it is also an

---

[11] See Hussin Mutalib, "Constitutional-electoral reforms and politics in Singapore", *Legislative Studies Quarterly*, 27(4), pp. 659–672, 2002.

excellent strategic approach to recruit new PAP members into Parliament. The Opposition, which lacks a large pool of talent, has generally been unwilling to compete head-on with senior PAP candidates. For instance, key opposition leaders such as Chiam See Tong and Low Thia Khiang preferred to compete in Single Member Constituencies (SMCs) and to their credit, were successful. Still, to the credit of the opposition parties, the 2011 general elections was much more vibrant as the Opposition made a credible effort of mounting a large-scale challenge against the PAP across the various GRCs, including succeeding, for the first time, in capturing a GRC at Aljunied. In the 2015 general elections, the Workers' Party (WP) retained its hold over Aljunied GRC.

The government has also argued that the GRC system has compelled all political parties and MPs to be conscious of the multiracial character of Singapore. According to Prime Minister Lee, the GRC system "puts pressure on us [to think of multiracial Singapore] and the PAP but I think it is the right system."[12] For the government, the GRC has an added bonus: it works together with the system of Town Councils (TCs). Due to the linkage between the GRC and TC, Prime Minister Lee argued that it will ensure responsible politics and compel the voters to be realistic.[13]

The GRC scheme clearly sets the Singapore model of government apart from the typical Westminster parliamentary system. The enlarged representation is a distinct political innovation that contrasts the traditional SMC which is a defining characteristic of the Westminster system. The electorate is unable to cast its vote for a particular candidate and has no choice but to accept all the candidates in a GRC team or reject the team entirely. Although accepting the merits of the GRC scheme to ensure minority representation, such a system also reduces the relationship between the electorate and its representatives, since the relationship has evolved from individual-to-individual to that of

---

[12] Zakir Hussain, "Changes to political system to prepare Singapore for long term: PM Lee Hsien Loong".

[13] Zakir Hussain, "Changes to political system to prepare Singapore for long term: PM Lee Hsien Loong".

the individual-to-team. A counter argument is that the electorate is still able to relate directly with the individual MP as the GRC is merely an electoral mechanism, with the normal MP-to-electorate relationship largely intact and unchanged in every other sense.

The Elected President system

The role of the President of Singapore has been traditionally ceremonial. Since 1984, with the Opposition's success in breaking the PAP's complete control of Parliament, the ruling party began to seek ways to limit the intrusion of the Opposition and neutralise its impact on Singapore politics. Chief amongst the PAP's concern was to safeguard its vast national reserves in the event an irresponsible government comes to power in Singapore. Another key area of concern was over key appointments in public service. By 1991, the PAP government released a *White Paper* stating the creation of an EP tasked with the duty to guard Singapore's financial reserves. The analogy given for the EP was that a 'two-key' mechanism was needed for the release of Singapore's reserves. The Prime Minister as the head of government would hold one key while the EP would hold the second key to the lock.

For the government, the EP was not an executive position but held custodial duties. According to Prime Minister Lee, the President, in addition to being the Head of State, "would exercise custodial powers over the spending of past reserves, and key appointments in the public service."[14] A council of presidential advisers was also created to assist the President in carrying out his tasks. The President has no executive or policy making role as this remains "the prerogative of the elected Government commanding the majority in Parliament."[15]

Not surprisingly, the EP was greeted with much cynicism when Ong Teng Cheong, a long-time PAP Deputy Prime Minister, resigned from the party to contest in the first EP in 1993. Although there was a

---

[14] Zakir Hussain, "Changes to political system to prepare Singapore for long term: PM Lee Hsien Loong".
[15] Zakir Hussain, "Changes to political system to prepare Singapore for long term: PM Lee Hsien Loong".

contestation for the post in 1993, the other contender, Chua Kim Yeow, was very much a reluctant candidate, pushed into action "after some arm-twisting by PAP stalwarts, Goh Keng Swee and Richard Hu" (Mauzy and Milne, 2002, p. 153). Ong easily won the presidency.

To the credit of Ong as the newly elected EP, he pushed for a much clearer role of the EP. Ong was at odds with his former colleagues over the level of information and authority over Singapore's reserves that he should have as the EP. Not surprisingly, the PAP government in 1994 began to review the powers of the EP. In the later years of Ong's tenure, the differences that he had with the PAP government over the role, functions and independence of the EP intensified and were widely covered in the local press. However, Ong did not seek a second term due to ill health and the office of the EP was won uncontested by S.R. Nathan, a distinguished civil servant and former diplomat. Nathan held the office for two consecutive terms.

The EP, in essence, is clearly an innovation of the Singapore's government. However, the PAP by limiting the discretionary powers of the EP has reduced the role of the EP and returned the role of the presidency to that of a predominantly functional role. Even though the EP can act robustly under certain circumstances, this is something that has never been exercised and is yet to be tested. With a set of stringent criteria in place for the selection of EP candidates, few are able to fulfill the requirements. Moreover, the EP is compelled to accept the advice of the Presidential Advisory Committee, a committee appointed by the PAP government, essentially a check by the executive on the EP.

While for long, the PAP and probably the public assumed that the EP was a position created for good governance and stability in national politics, it came as a shock when the PAP supported candidate for the presidential election in August 2011 barely won the presidency. Four candidates, all linked to the government in one way or another, contested and the former Deputy Prime Minister, Tony Tan, essentially the PAP's candidate, only garnered 35.2% of the total votes. His closest rival, the highly popular Tan Cheng Bock, a former PAP MP, garnered 34.85% of the total votes. The other two candidates, Tan Jee Say and Tan Kin Lian secured 25.04% and 4.91% of the total votes, respectively. While the public unhappiness with the PAP, first expressed in the May 2011 general elections was now translated into anti-PAP sentiments in the presidential elections, it also signaled that the PAP could not take its dominance for granted.

The 2016 political-electoral adjustments

On 27 January 2016, Singapore's Prime Minister Lee proposed a constitutional amendment that would alter the status and rights of the NCMPs and the EP. The number of NCMPs would be increased from nine to 12 in the next general elections. The NCMPs would also be given the same voting rights as MPs. At the same time, the President would remain an elected office. However, a Constitutional Commission, chaired by the Chief Justice, would review three key areas relating to the EP. The three areas include: "updating the eligibility criteria for presidential candidates, strengthening the Council of Presidential Advisers and ensuring minorities have a chance to be elected."[16] The report of the commission was quickly to prepare for the country's presidential election that was later held in September 2017. Referred to as the 'reserved EP', the idea was to ensure that minorities were, on a regular basis given a chance to become the country's highest office holders. As no Malay had been President since the death of Yusof Ishak in 1970, the 2017 presidential election was reserved for a Malay which was eventually won by Halimah Yacob. The position and powers of the NMPs would remain unchanged. The Prime Minister also promised to have smaller GRCs and increase the number of SMCs at the next general elections.

Conclusion

Clearly, the political system in practice today is very much different from the one inherited from the British colonisers. While remaining essentially

---

[16] Zakir Hussain, "Changes to political system to prepare Singapore for long term: PM Lee Hsien Loong".

a British Westminster parliamentary system, various innovations, such as the GRCs, NCMPs, NMPs and EP, especially reserved EP, have been introduced to ensure a certain degree of political resilience in the system. A key factor in this regard is to reflect the multiracial and multi-religious architecture of Singapore. While democracy is a useful functioning mechanism, however, in an overwhelmingly Chinese-majority Singapore, where 75% of the population is made up of ethnic Chinese, political stabilisers have been introduced to ensure that the political system exudes a certain degree of fair and representative democracy *a la Singapore*. Through various innovations, at any one time, there will always be ethnic representatives from all the racial groups, Chinese, Malays, Indians and Others, thereby ensuring and guaranteeing ethnic peace and harmony. To that extent, through adroit constitutional amendments and political practices, wise political reforms have been injected into the system to ensure political stability, especially at a time of rising ethno-nationalism worldwide, thereby acting as powerful political stabilisers in Singapore.

The need for robust political stabilisers is all the more urgent in view of the rising ethno-religious nationalism worldwide, escalating cyber-attacks on public and private platforms, and the greater propensity to use fake news to shape a country's national political agenda. While Singapore's racial, religious and language fault lines are known, the high internet penetration of the society has also made it extremely vulnerable to subversion by state and non-state actors in the region and beyond. Today, states have the potential to use 'hired guns and fake new mills' to harm the domestic stability of another state.[17] Indonesia experienced this type of attack with the 'Ahok' political assassination campaign launched by Saracen, known as a notorious fake news factory in Indonesia.[18] In view of these potential threats with Singapore as a potential 'sandbox for subversion', the emplacement of a robust and resilient political stabilisers and mechanisms are

---

[17] See Kelly Ng, "Experts mixed on whether fake-news laws can protect society from 'threats of our time'", *Today*, 21 March 2018.
[18] Kelly Ng, "Experts mixed on whether fake-news laws can protect society from 'threats of our time'".

a *sine quo non* for the long-term stability of a perpetually vulnerable Singapore. It is thus equally important for Singapore citizens to be aware of these threats and challenges so that they do not succumb to fake news or attempts to exploit domestic fault lines to divide the society through misinformation and disinformation from within and abroad.

Chapter 5

Housing as Asset Building in Singapore

Hongbo Jia and S Vasoo

Introduction

The prioritisation and importance of an asset-based welfare policy developed by Michael Sherraden[1] led to great attention being paid by scholars and policymakers in the last two decades in the area. Asset-based welfare policy, which is a kind of developmental social policy,[2] emphasised the importance of individuals holding assets as part of individual welfare and well-being.[3] Housing, one of the most important forms of asset, can enhance the daily life quality of family members due to its diverse functions for habitation, shelter, family life, social interaction, asset reserve and assistance in business. Housing property, a valuable asset-building tool, contributes to keeping housing prices more stable, leading to many studies focusing on the relationship between homeownership and asset building directly or

---

[1] Michael Sherraden, *Assets and the poor: A new American welfare policy* (New York: M.E. Sharpe, 1991).

[2] Marc Mannes, Eugene C. Roehlkepartain and Peter L. Benson, "Unleashing the power of community to strengthen the well-being of children, youth, and families: An asset-building approach", *Child Welfare, 84*(2), pp. 233–250, 2005.

[3] Rajiv Prabhakar, "What is the future for asset-based welfare?", *Public Policy Research, 16*(1), pp. 51–56, 2009.

indirectly.[4] In recent years, some Western countries regard homeownership as a positive way to alleviate economic hardship and to offset insufficient pension.[5]

As a small open city-state, Singapore has a high proportion of homeownership. Most Singaporeans own public housing flats from the Housing and Development Board (HDB), making Singapore a model for intervention by the state in housing areas across the world. This has also raised great interest for academic enquiry to explore whether and how to realise asset building by homeownership. Beng Huat Chua[6] examines the operations, conditions, consequences and contradictions of public housing as asset for retirement in Singapore. Yong Tu, Sock-Yong Phang, and Robert H. Edelstein and Sau Kim Lum[7] focus on public homeownership's effect on wealth formation

---

[4] Richard Ronald and John Doling, "Shifting East Asian approaches to home ownership and the housing welfare pillar", *European Journal of Housing Policy*, 10(3), pp. 233–254, 2010; Richard Ronald, "Between investment, asset and use consumption: The meanings of homeownership in Japan", *Housing Studies*, 23(2), pp. 233–251, 2008; Gary V. Engelhardt, Michael D. Eriksen, William G. Gale and Gregory B. Mills, "What are the social benefits of homeownership?: Experimental evidence for low-income households", *Journal of Urban Economics*, 67(3), pp. 249–258, 2010; Val Colic-Peisker, Rachel Ong and Gavin Wood, "Asset poverty, precarious housing and ontological security in older age: An Australian case study", *European Journal of Housing Policy*, 15(2), pp. 167–186, 2015; Janneke Toussaint and Marja Elsinga, "Exploring 'housing asset-based welfare': Can the UK be held up as an example for Europe?", *Housing Studies*, 24(5), pp. 669–692, 2009; and Wouter P.C. van Gent, "Housing policy as a lever for change?: The politics of welfare, assets and tenure", *Housing Studies*, 25(5), pp. 735–753, 2010.

[5] James Lee, "Housing policy and asset building: Exploring the role of home ownership in East Asian social policy", *China Journal of Social Work*, 6(2), pp. 104–117, 2013.

[6] Beng Huat Chua, "Navigating between limits: The future of public housing in Singapore", *Housing Studies*, 29(4), pp. 520–533, 2014; Beng Huat Chua, "Financialising public housing as an asset for retirement in Singapore", *International Journal of Housing Policy*, 15(1), pp. 27–42, 2015.

[7] Yong Tu, "Public homeownership, housing finance and socioeconomic development in Singapore", *Review of Urban & Regional Development Studies*, 11(2), pp. 100–113, 1999; Sock-Yong Phang, "Housing policy, wealth formation and the Singapore economy", *Housing Studies* 16(4), pp. 443–459, 2001; and Robert H.

and economic development in Singapore. Ashok Bardhan *et al.*, Tai-Chee Wong and Adriel Yap[8] and Yong Tu, Lanny K. Kwee and Belinda Yuen[9] analyse how public homeownership accelerated the upward mobility behaviour of Singapore households to private homeownership. S Vasoo and James Lee, Loo Lee Sim, Ming Yu Shi and Sheng Han Sun[10] and Treena Wu and Angelique Chan[11] explore the role of public homeownership for social development such as ethnic integration in Singapore.

In all of the aforementioned studies, the authors show evidence that there was a close relationship, either positive or negative, between public homeownership and asset building in Singapore, especially relating to financial asset building. However, this is only part of the story. Few scholars have examined the role of homeownership to human asset building in Singapore. Moreover, in the past decade, the existing literature has not paid enough attention on the impact homeownership on social asset building in Singapore except for a few research articles. As argued by Wai-Fong Ting,[12] the concept of asset

---

Edelstein and Sau Kim Lum, "House prices, wealth effects, and the Singapore macroeconomy", *Journal of Housing Economics 13*(4), pp. 342–367, 2004.

[8] Ashok Deo Bardhan, Rajarshi Datta, Robert H. Edelstein and Lum Sau Kim, "A tale of two sectors: Upward mobility and the private housing market in Singapore", *Journal of Housing Economics,* 12(2), pp. 83–105, 2003; and Tai-Chee Wong and Adriel Yap, "From universal public housing to meeting the increasing aspiration for private housing in Singapore", *Habitat International* 27(3), pp. 361–380, 2003.

[9] Yong Tu, Lanny K. Kwee and Belinda Yuen, "An empirical analysis of Singapore households' upgrading mobility behaviour: From public homeownership to private homeownership", *Habitat International,* 29(3), pp. 511–525, 2005.

[10] S Vasoo and James Lee, "Singapore: Social development, housing and the Central Provident Fund", *International Journal of Social Welfare, 10*(4), pp. 276–283, 2001; and Loo Lee Sim, Ming Yu Shi and Sheng Han Sun, "Public housing and ethnic integration in Singapore", *Habitat International* 27(2), pp. 293–307, 2003.

[11] Treena Wu and Angelique Chan, "Families, friends, and the neighborhood of older adults: Evidence from public housing in Singapore", *Journal of Aging Research,* 2012(3), pp. 1–7, 2012.

[12] Wai-Fong Ting, "Asset building and livelihood rebuilding in post-disaster Sichuan, China", *China Journal of Social Work, 6*(3), pp. 190–207, 2013.

should include three types, namely financial asset, human asset and social asset. Asset building may increase an individual's social, economic, psychological and political capabilities and influence the person's long-term saving and investment behaviour. Rental housing meets the needs of consumptive behaviour by solving the housing demand but does not play the role of asset building.

The aim of this study is to explore the influences of Singapore's housing programme, which uniquely has the highest public home-ownership, to financial, human and social asset building in Singapore. No analysis of this issue, to our knowledge, has been undertaken. The next section is on the development of homeownership programme in Singapore. The following section will review the role of homeownership on financial, human and social asset building, before concluding the study.

Development of Homeownership Programmes in Singapore

Singapore has the highest rate of homeownership in the world,[13] with most of Singaporeans owning their HDB flats. Two years after acquiring self-government in 1959 from the British colonial administration, Singapore led by the People's Action Party (PAP) established the HDB in 1961 to improve the living conditions of the newly enfranchised citizens, whose previous housing was seriously congested and had an unhygienic physical environment. At the early start, one-room, two-room and three-room HDB flats were built, provided as rental housing for low-income families to cope with the severe housing shortage. With the development of HDB's strategy, the government changed its housing policy in 1964 and decided to concentrate on homeownership scheme with an aim to encourage the majority of lower- and middle-income groups to become flat owners of 99-year leasehold flats. Due to strict conditions such as identity of buyers, income ceiling and down payment of household, there was a slow

---

[13] Mukul G. Asher, *Compulsory savings in Singapore: An alternative to the welfare state* (NCPA Policy Report No. 198, 1995) pp. 1–15.

growth for the selling of flats and no significant increase in the number of dwellings sold even when income ceilings were raised and smaller households allowed to purchase public housing.[14]

The government allowed the transfer of individual Central Provident Fund (CPF) accumulation into public homeownership in 1968 for the initial down payment, monthly mortgage repayment and other ancillary transaction costs of purchasing HDB flats, which enhanced the public homeownership rate significantly. Economic growth and income improvement provided the possibility for government to promote public homeownership further in 1970s with measures such as raised income ceiling of household for purchasing HDB apartments, giving tenants more options to buy their rented HDB apartments. Meanwhile, the Housing and Urban Development Company Pte Ltd (HUDC) was established by the government in 1974 to create public housing programmes for the middle-income group.

The public housing policies in the 1970s created a peak in the applications for public housing in both the rental and owner-occupier sectors.[15] With HUDC integrated into HDB in 1982, new HDB public housing programmes have covered low- and middle-income groups, with the HDB focusing on promoting HDB flat owners to sell and upgrade their apartments. A cycle of 'buy/sell/repurchase' was created within public housing homeownership by permitting tenants to sell the flats on an open market, instead of selling it back to the HDB, and repurchase a new subsidised flat from the HDB,[16] which further provided incentives to expand homeownership in the 1980s.

In 1993, the change of mortgage financing policy boosted the HDB resale housing market. Additionally, the private housing market developed quickly, partly attributed by the relaxed governmental control of land and the birth of the Approved Residential Properties

---

[14] Yong Tu, "Public homeownership, housing finance and socioeconomic development in Singapore".

[15] Yong Tu, "Public homeownership, housing finance and socioeconomic development in Singapore".

[16] Beng Huat Chua, "Navigating between limits: The future of public housing in Singapore".

Scheme (ARPS) in 1981 to permit the use of CPF savings for paying back of buyers' housing loans, which in turn swelled the whole housing market prices in Singapore. During the Asian financial crisis in 1997, the pressure of the downward economy caused a reduction in CPF contributions and a decrease in the financing capacity of CPF savings for housing. Thus, to keep homeownership stable, extra low-interest loans were offered by HDB to support flat buyers who had difficulty in paying off the mortgage. Entering into the 21st century, high, stable and affordable homeownership, the clearest feature in Singapore, is still a priority of the government's housing programme.

As a summary, homeownership in Singapore has increased hugely in the past five decades. The General Household Survey 2015 showed that homeownership in Singapore stood at 90.8% in 2015, of which about 80.1% of households lived in HDB dwellings, and Key Statistics HDB Annual Report 2015/2016 estimated the percentage of Singapore resident population living in HDB sold flats to be 79%. The housing property increased several folds since 1960s.

The Role of Homeownership in Asset Building

Homeownership means that owners have the unique right to use their housing, which will result in many changes in assets. Asset building is the process of supporting and encouraging one to acquire the ability to accumulate, develop and preserve all types of asset. This section attempts to discuss the linkage of homeownership to financial, human and social asset building from the perspective of asset-based welfare policy while evaluating the real outcomes of homeownership to financial, human and social asset building in Singapore.

Financial asset building

Mechanism

Homeownership is the main engine triggering a mechanism towards financial asset building. Public housing in Singapore has been considered and operated as both an economic development tool and a solution to the lack of shelter.[17] People who own HDB flats must work harder to improve their income to pay for their installments. As the monthly mortgage could only be paid with a regular monthly income, homeownership imposed a discipline on workers to stay in regular employment in the formal sector of the economy.[18] On one hand, working harder contributes to higher productivity and economic growth, which leads to more sufficient revenue and governmental support for homeownership. On the other hand, working harder is good to earn higher income and higher CPF savings, which makes HDB flat owners more qualified to purchase the bigger flats. This will make it possible to enhance demand and make it affordable to purchase better public housing. The asset development perspective is illustrated in Figure 5.1, which provides a schematic view of the

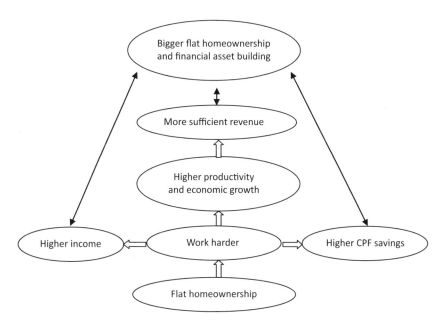

Figure 5.1. The schematic view of financial asset enhancement by homeownership

---

[17] Brian Field and George Ofori, "Housing stress and the role of the state", *Habitat International*, *13*(3), pp. 125–138, 1989.
[18] Beng Huat Chua, "Navigating between limits: The future of public housing in Singapore".

financial asset enhancement cycle through homeownership. Homeownership triggers apartment owners to save and attain higher financial asset levels in future on the condition of value appreciation in public housing. Whether attaining a higher financial asset level will be sustainable is questionable, which needs to be addressed and is often tied to political stability and sustainable social and economic development.

Outcome

The necessary condition of homeownership that contributes to financial asset building is through value appreciation in housing. The basic condition of value appreciation in housing is that the yearly growth rate for price of HDB apartments has to keep up with the annual inflation rate, not to be lower at least but preferably be higher than the annual inflation rate. Economic recession, a naturally progressive loss of estate value, and a gradually shorter remaining lease, may cause a reduction in the housing value. The Singapore government is committed to asset appreciation by adopting several measures such as the upgrading scheme, and introducing a pricing formula for new flats against the market pricing. It tracks the gap between growth rate for price of HDB apartments and inflation rate yearly as an index to measure the empirical outcomes of homeownership to financial asset building.

Considering the availability of data, this study uses the HDB Resale Price Index from 1990 to 2016 as the substitution variables to price of HDB apartments. The result of gap between growth rate for price of HDB apartments and inflation rate yearly is shown in Figure 5.2. It demonstrates that there was a considerable appreciation from 1991 to 1997 generally with about 26% average gap between the growth rate for price of HDB apartments and the inflation rate yearly, especially in 1993 when there was an appreciable peak. However, the 1997 Asian financial crisis caused a huge depreciation in housing value. Since then, despite a gradual recovery of housing appreciation, the trend of high housing appreciation has ceased and the housing appreciation rate fluctuated around zero, with the

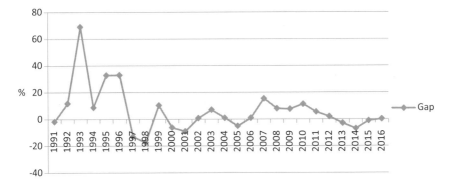

Figure 5.2. The gap between growth rate for price of HDB apartments and inflation rate

Note: The yearly HDB Resale Price Index to calculate the gap between growth rate for price of HDB apartments and inflation rate is the annual 4th Quarter Resale Price Index.
Source: Calculated in light of Resale Price Index (RPI) (1990–2016) and World Economic Outlook Database (IMF).

average gap between growth rate for price of HDB apartments and inflation rate yearly is about 0.4% from 1997 to 2016.

These findings highlight that one should be cautious when linking homeownership to financial asset building. In the long run, whether owners can acquire financial asset building through homeownership depends on the time when holders buy and sell the apartments. For example, homeowners who bought and sold apartments between 1991 to 2016 would generally see financial asset enhancement due to the average gap between growth rate for price of HDB apartments and inflation rate yearly to be about 6.2%. The same thing happened for owners who bought and sold apartments between 1991 to 1996. However, owners who bought and sold apartments between 1997 and 2016 had no obvious consequences on financial asset building. Therefore, whether there is a sustainable real appreciation in housing value is the key to financial asset building. Homeownership, the engine triggering a mechanism towards financial asset building, cannot assure that the goal will be inevitably attained. However, the outcome of homeownership facilitates the mobility to owning bigger flat is evident. With regard to the outcomes of moving to bigger HDB flats, the trend for HDB households has been to move from smaller to larger flats and the number of households living in bigger four-room and five-room flats has risen quite significantly. As demonstrated by the HDB Sample Household Survey 2013, there was 41.1% HDB resident population living in four-room flats and 26.6% in five-room flats in 2013. The corresponding figure in 1980 was 14% and 5%, respectively (Census of population 1980), with the biggest increase taking place from 1980 to 2010.

Human asset building

Mechanism

Human asset is often said to be intangible and one encompassing such aspects as the stock of competence, knowledge, experience, skill and health, which is arguably assessed to be of social and economic value. A number of studies have addressed the positive relationship between better housing conditions and increasing health.[19] Homeownership of

---

[19] Rima R. Habib, Ziyad Mahfoud, Mona Fawaz, Shiraz H. Basma and Joumana S. Yeretzian, "Housing quality and ill health in a disadvantaged urban community", *Public Health*, *123*(2), pp. 174–181, 2009; Tansel Yilmazer, Patryk Babiarz and Feng Liu, "The impact of diminished housing wealth on health in the United States: Evidence from the great recession", *Social Science & Medicine*, *130C*, pp. 234–241, 2015; Ana M. Novoa, Julia Ward, Davide Malmusi, Fernando Díaz, Mercè Darnell and Carme Trilla, *et al.*, "How substandard dwellings and housing affordability problems are associated with poor health in a vulnerable population during the economic recession of the late 2000s", *International Journal for Equity in Health*, *14*(1), pp. 1–11, 2015; Rebecca T. Brown, Yinghui Miao, Susan L. Mitchell, Monica Bharel, Mitkumar Patel and Kevin L. Ard, *et al.*, "Health outcomes of obtaining housing among older homeless adults", *American Journal of Public Health*, *105*(7), pp. 1482–1488, 2015; Gary Adamkiewicz, John D. Spengler, Amy E. Harley, Anne Stoddard, May Yang and Marty Alvarez-Reeves, *et al.*, "Environmental conditions in low-income urban housing: Clustering and associations with self-reported health", *American Journal of Public Health*, *104*(9), pp. 1650–1656, 2014; Matt Egan, Srinivasa Vittal Katikireddi, Ade Kearns, Carol Tannahill, Martins Kalacs and Lyndal Bond, "Health effects of neighborhood demolition and housing improvement: A prospective controlled study of 2 natural experiments in urban renewal", *American Journal of Public Health*, *103*(6), 2013, pp. 47–53; and F. Breinig, T. Sendzik,

HDB flats, a type of formal and stable housing holding, contributes to health improvement, as was demonstrated by Sarah A. Burgard, Kristin S. Seefeldt and Sarah Zelner[20] that housing stability has positive effects on health. Owning one's home can confer greater feelings of security or prestige than social or private renting, and is often used as an indicator of greater long-term command over resources,[21] which has psycho-social impact on health. If one is healthy, it is a human asset, followed by a triggered mechanism with the higher income, higher CPF savings, higher productivity and economic growth, higher income, and finally the ability to access to bigger flats and the better human asset building as illustrated in Figure 5.3. In summary, the effect of homeownership on health helps people to be productive in sustainable social and economic endeavours which enable them to participate in the homeownership scheme cycle.

Outcome

The homeownership scheme in Singapore does implement diverse measures to promote housing conditions which affect people's physiological and psychological health. Prior to 1960s, Singaporeans lived in bad housing conditions of either urban 'shophouse' rows or 'kampong', informal settlements of wooden houses with thatched roofs. Nowadays, as aforementioned, the HDB Sample Household Survey 2013 showed that the HDB resident population who lived in four-room flats and five-room flats are 41.1% and 26.6% respectively, accounting for a total of 67.7% of all HDB resident population. There

---

K. Eisfeld and M.J. Schmitt, "The health impacts of housing improvement: A systematic review of intervention studies from 1887 to 2007", *American Journal of Public Health*, *99 Supplement 3*(S3), pp. S681–S692, 2009.

[20] Sarah A. Burgard, Kristin S. Seefeldt and Sarah Zelner, "Housing instability and health: Findings from the Michigan recession and recovery study", *Social Science & Medicine*, *75*(12), pp. 2215–2224, 2012.

[21] Marcia Gibson, Mark Petticrew, Clare Bambra, Amanda J. Sowden, Kath E. Wright and Margaret Whitehead "Housing and health inequalities: A synthesis of systematic reviews of interventions aimed at different pathways linking housing and health", *Health & Place*, *17*(1), pp. 175–184, 2011.

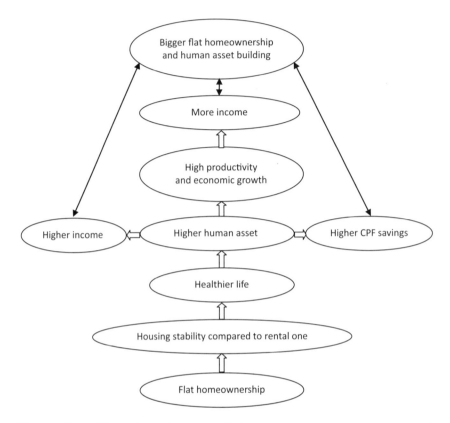

Figure 5.3. The schematic view of human asset enhancement through homeownership

is a significant progress in housing conditions. Based on anecdotal evidence, residents who lived in a better and cleaner environment would be less susceptible to transmittable diseases. The study by J.W.L. Kleevens[22] showed that after moving from worse to better sanitary conditions, Ascaris-infections were reduced by half in a six-month period and Trichuris-infections (worm infestations) within one year. In order to completely assess outcomes of homeownership to human asset building (represented by health hereby), the correlation

---

[22] J.W.L. Kleevens, *Housing and health in a tropical city: A selective study in Singapore, 1964–1967* (Netherlands: Kominklijke Van Gorcm & Comp, 1972).

Table 5.1. The data of AP and LE from 1980 to 2013 (Selected year)

Year	AP	LE
1980	19.0	72.1
1987	38.9	74.5
1993	49.4	76.1
1998	59.4	77.3
2003	66.5	79.1
2008	67.7	80.9
2013	67.7	82.4

Source: The data of AP was computed from Census of Population 1980 and HDB Sample Household Survey 2013. The data of LE is from Singapore Department of Statistics.

between upgrading of housing conditions and health status can be computed. The upgrading of housing conditions can be measured indirectly by the aggregate percentage (abbreviated with AP hereafter) of HDB resident population who lived in four-room flats and five-room flats. Generally, health status can be measured by life expectancy at birth (abbreviated with LE hereafter). The data from 1980 to 2013 (selected year) are listed in Table 5.1. By computing, the correlation coefficient for AP and LE is 0.938, which means that percentage of bigger homeownership flats by homeownership is highly correlated to better health. Therefore, a conclusion can be drawn that homeownership is helpful to human asset building represented by health.

Social asset building

Mechanism

Social asset or capital defined as connections among individuals–social networks and the norms of reciprocity and trustworthiness that arise from them.[23] Social asset covers support networks which include both formal organisations such as community groups, voluntary welfare organisations and informal groups like friends, relatives and neighbours. Social capital is different from other forms of capital because it is contained in the relationships between actors and is therefore not possessed by the actors themselves.[24] These social assets are associated with norms of reciprocity and add value to one's social life.[25] There are vast literatures focused on the effective social value of housing.[26] Considering the multifaceted values embedded in different national cultures, the path of housing contributing to social asset has no complete uniformity. Homeownership plays a key role towards social asset building in Singapore as revealed in Figure 5.4. On one hand, the longer residents live in the estate, the higher they should score on social capital.[27] Homeownership augments housing stability compared to (home) rental, which promotes further family and kinship enhancement and better community bonding. On the other hand, homeownership accompanied with an ethnic distribution system in HDB flats in Singapore fortifies harmonious ethnic relations. Three factors induced from homeownership, namely family and kinship enhancement, better community bonding, and more harmonious ethnic relations all bring about social asset building.

---

[23] Robert D. Putman, *Bowling alone: The collapse and revival of American community* (New York: Simon & Schuster, 2000).

[24] James S. Coleman, "Social capital in the creation of human capital", *American Journal of Sociology, 94*, pp. 95–120, 1988.

[25] Robert D. Putnam, "Social capital: Measurement and consequence", *Canadian Journal of Policy Research, 2*, pp. 41–51, 2001.

[26] Ed Ferrari, "The social value of housing in straitened times: The view from England", *Housing Studies, 30*(4), pp. 514–534, 2015; Nick Gallent, "The social value of second homes in rural communities", *Housing Theory & Society, 31*(2), pp. 174–191, 2014; and Richard Lang and Andreas Novy, "Cooperative housing and social cohesion: the role of linking social capital", *European Planning Studies, 22*(8), pp. 1744–1764, 2014.

[27] Seong-Kyu Ha, "Housing, social capital and community development in Seoul", *Cities, 27*(3), S35–S42, 2010.

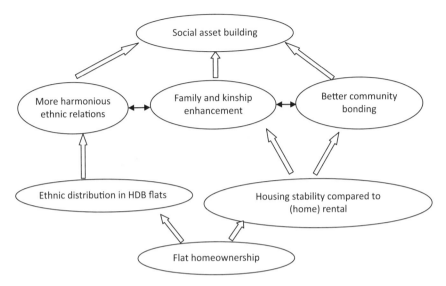

Figure 5.4. The schematic view of social asset enhancement through homeownership

Outcome

Measuring social capital is a complex task, in part, because we know very little about how it actually operates at a micro-level.[28] There are three kinds of social capital, namely bonding social capital, bridging social capital and linking social capital.[29] Homeownership in Singapore generally contributes to all three types of social capitals in both horizontal and vertical aspects. Homeownership is conducive to family

[28] Robert D. Putman, *Bowling alone: The collapse and revival of American community.*

[29] Ross J. Gittell and Avis Vidal, "Community organizing: Building social capital as a development strategy", *Contemporary Sociology, 29*(2), pp. 352–354, 2000; Robert D. Putman, *Bowling alone: The collapse and revival of American community;* Alan Middleton, Alan Murie and Rick Groves, "Social capital and neighbourhoods that work", *Urban Studies, 42*(42), pp. 1711–1738, 2005; Organisation for Economic Co-operation and Development (OECD), *The well-being of nations: The role of human and social capital* (Paris, France: The Author, 2001); and Michael Woolcock, "The place of social capital in understanding social and economic outcomes", *ISUMA Canadian Journal of Policy Research, 2*(1), pp. 11–17, 2001.

and kinship enhancement. Family cohesion is considered to be the core strength of Singapore's society.[30] The positive family kinship comes from good communication and the mutual care and support from family members. Homeownership, a scheme which creates higher housing stability for owners than for tenants, encourages family members to live under one roof to interact with each other harmoniously.

Moreover, a bigger HDB flat attributed to the homeownership programme can provide enough space for personal privacy among family members. Stella R. Quah[31] made a local study on the adequacy of space and living arrangements for the internal density of households in Singapore from 1940s to 1990s and found that family stress has decreased notably. It is observed that the average household size had declined from 6.2 persons in 1968 to 3.4 persons in 2013 due to transformation of the household structure from extended family to nuclear family, with the private space for each family member increasing relatively. Considering the trends of owning bigger HDB flats, the double beneficial effect of protecting the privacy of family members was achieved. The "Importance of and Satisfaction with Family Life by Year" conducted by the HDB Sample Household Survey is a good indirect index to measure the consequence of homeownership to family and kinship enhancement. Findings from the survey showed that the importance of and satisfaction with family life for both younger married residents with parents and older residents with married children continued to increase over the past decade, indicating the significance of homeownership to family and kinship enhancement (Figure 5.5).

Many countries have also paid attention to housing and ethnic integration.[32] Ethnic relations cannot be ignored in the context of

---

[30] Raj K. Vasil, *Governing Singapore: Democracy and national development* (Singapore: South Wind Production, 2000).

[31] Stella R. Quah, *Family in Singapore: Sociological perspectives* (Singapore: Times Academic Press, 1998).

[32] Hugo Priemus, "Redifferentiation of the urban housing stock in the Netherlands: A strategy to prevent spatial segregation?", *Housing Studies, 13*(3), pp. 301–310, 1998; John M. Goering, "Opening housing opportunities: Changing Federal

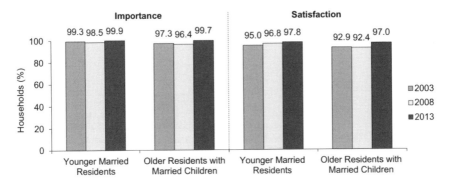

Figure 5.5. Importance of and satisfaction with family life by year
Source: HDB Sample Household Survey 2013.

Singapore's social and political landscape. There is enough evidence to suggest that homeownership is conducive to a more harmonious inter-ethnic relation. Brian W. Hodder[33] shows that Singapore was "a sociologically immature city where racial, tribal and economic divisions [were] still quite sharp." Just not too long ago, race riots happened in 1964 and 1969 and those were to some extent fanned by the early colonial policy directed at segregated living of different ethnic groups in various residential enclaves which comprised separately of Chinese, Malay and Indian living much on their own.

However, these ethnic enclaves were re-organised when HDB mounted its Ethnic Integration Policy (EIP) in 1989 to prevent the formation of ethnic enclaves. The ethnic distribution in HDB estates and neighbourhoods is based on the percentage of each ethnic group in Singapore's total population to ensure a balanced mix of different ethnic groups in HDB estates. This public housing policy arrangement

---

Housing Policy in the United States", in Frederick Boal (ed.), *Ethnicity and housing: Accommodating the differences* (England: Ashgate, 2000); and Maurice Blanc, "Housing segregation and the poor: New trends in French social rented housing", *Housing Studies*, 8(3), pp. 207–214, 1993.
[33] Brian W. Hodder, "Racial groupings in Singapore", *Malayan Journal of Tropical Geography*, 1, pp. 25–36, 1953.

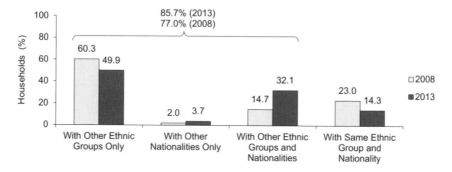

Figure 5.6.　Engagement in inter-ethnic/nationality interaction by year
Source: HDB Sample Household Survey 2013.

has the added role of promoting inter-ethnic relations, understanding and harmony, thereby succeeding in reducing the intensity of the ethnic enclaves while increasing social integration.[34] Another evidence to demonstrate better inter-ethnic relations is borne-out by the HDB Household Surveys on an item "Engagement in Inter-Ethnic/ Nationality Interaction by Year". As depicted in Figure 5.6, between 2008 and 2013, more residents engaged in inter-ethnic/nationality interactions. In fact, the proportion of residents who had interacted with neighbours of other ethnic groups and/or nationalities had increased from 77% in 2008 to 85.7% in 2013. Singapore's housing policy has enhanced social integration as different income and ethnic groups are housed together, and thus live and interact with one another.[35]

Community bonding is another concern of implementation for public housing programme. Through community development activities, the interaction among community members can create a unique social bond that fosters group cohesion, group identity and

---

[34] Loo Lee Sim, Ming Yu Shi and Sheng Han Sun, "Public housing and ethnic integration in Singapore".

[35] S Vasoo and James Lee, "Singapore: Social development, housing and the Central Provident Fund".

cooperativeness.[36] Residents of a community who are able to engage in daily contacts have the greatest potential to help generate social capital compared to those who do not.[37] The results of public housing programme for promoting community bonding in Singapore can be measured by three dimensions. The first dimension is the degree of neighbourliness. HDB Sample Household Survey 2013 showed that neighbourly ties were still alive and strong due to the fact that almost all residents were engaged in exchanging greetings and casual conversation. There is no doubt that living stability attributed to homeownership such as housing rule requiring owners of flats to have the minimum occupation period (MOP) has some positive influence on neighbourhood bonding. The second aspect is the sense of attachment to the community. This sense arises when people have a lively awareness of a familiar environment, a ritual repetition, and a sense of fellowship based on the shared experience.[38]

As is evident in Figure 5.7, HDB Sample Household Survey 2013 showed that the sense of belonging increased over the years. The proportion of residents who had developed a sense of belonging to their towns/estates continued to rise from 79.1% in 1993 to 98.8% in 2013. Moreover, HDB Sample Household Survey 2013 also revealed that the sense of belonging increased with the length of residence. Homeownership caused housing stability which played a significant role for increasing the sense of community belonging.

The third aspect is the community engagement that is measured by participation in community activities. The strong sense of belonging and community sentiments have also facilitated residents' participation in various community and social organisations such as Residents' Committees (RCs), Community Clubs/Centres (CCs), Voluntary Welfare Organisations (VWOs) and Community

---

[36] Richard E. Leakey, *Origins* (New York: Rainbird, 1977).
[37] Nick Gallent, "The social value of second homes in rural communities".
[38] J.B. Jackson, "A sense of place, a sense of time", *Design Quarterly*, 8(164), pp. 24–27, 1995.

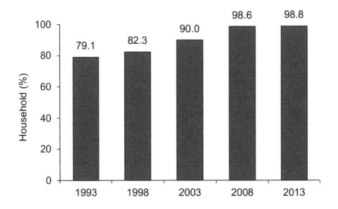

Figure 5.7.   Sense of belonging by year

Source: HDB Sample Household Survey 2013.

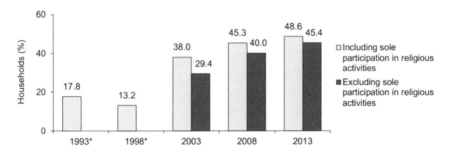

Figure 5.8.   Community participation over past 12 months by year

Note: * Prior to 2003, no differentiation was made between community and religious activities.
Source: HDB Sample Household Survey 2013.

Development Councils (CDCs). Many community activities such as commemorative celebrations, block parties, group tours, community festivals and interest group activities have been organised by community agencies and these increased the opportunities for residents to interact, trust, make friends and create a sense of belonging. HDB Sample Household Survey 2013 indicated that there was an increasing participation in community activities between 1993 and 2013, as showed in Figure 5.8.

Conclusion

Housing is one of the most important tools for asset-based welfare policy. High proportion of homeownership is the distinct feature of the housing market in Singapore. The effects of homeownership on asset building have raised a great degree of interest among scholars and policy makers. This study examined the influence of Singapore's housing programme on financial, human and social asset building. The role of homeownership in asset building was analysed to demonstrate the relationship of homeownership to financial, human and social asset building from the perspective of asset-based welfare policy and the real outcomes of homeownership to financial, human and social asset building in Singapore.

This study drew a number of conclusions. First, whether homeownership actually contributes to financial asset building is something that needs further exploration even though there is a theoretic triggering mechanism by homeownership for imposing a discipline to work harder for better financial asset building in Singapore. Keeping the economy stable, avoiding inflation and appreciating the housing value continuously are extremely important to financial asset building. The gap between growth rate for price of HDB apartments and inflation rate yearly is the direct index for measuring financial asset building.

Second, the homeownership scheme has improved housing conditions through upgrading oneself to own bigger HDB flats, resulting in better health, which is beneficial to human asset building in Singapore. Statistics has shown that the percentage of bigger homeownership flats by homeownership is highly correlated to better health.

Third, homeownership has significantly promoted social asset building in Singapore. Empirical evidence shows that homeownership not only contributed to family and kinship enhancement but also was conducive to ameliorating inter-ethnic relations and community bonding. The three conclusions show that homeownership in Singapore is more valuable for human asset building and social asset building than for financial asset building. From this point, the human and social value of homeownership needs to be extremely stressed in policy making.

The success of homeownership to asset building, particularly in human and social asset building, is attributable to several factors. First, a series of institutional arrangements towards homeownership enhancement are the key internal factors for promoting asset building. For example, individual cash saving, CPF contribution, HDB concessionary housing loans, bank loans and CPF housing grant (if eligible) are the multi-financial channels for easy access to home-ownership credits and all these financial provisions have helped lessen the burden of HDB flat owners. Open resale market transactions have allowed flat owners to sell flats to eligible buyers in the open market freely at an agreed price based on meeting some conditions such as MOP, which provides opportunity for flat owners to hold bigger HDB apartments or upgrade from public housing to private housing. Ethnic quota policy is applicable to the sale of new and resale flats and to all other housing priority schemes,[39] which aims at keeping the ethnic balance and this policy does affect pricing of flats, especially if they have to be sold to minority groups due to a relatively smaller demand. Numerous housing improvement programmes such as Main Upgrading Programme (MUP), Home Improvement Programme (HIP), Lift Upgrading Program (LUP) and Neighbourhood Renewal Programme (NRP) are helpful in appreciating the value of HDB flats for financial asset building by increasing the comparative advantages of the growth rate of housing price to inflation rate.

Second, having national capitalism as a political structure in Singapore contributes to homeownership as part of the asset-building strategy with a strong government support and intervention. The government's pursuit of public housing and the asset-specific

---

[39] Chih Hoong Sin, "Segregation and marginalisation within public housing: The disadvantaged in Bedok New Town, Singapore", *Housing Studies*, *17*(2), pp. 267–288, 2002.

elements of housing schemes are the principal sources of path dependence in Singapore housing policy.[40] The government can acquire low-cost land under the Land Acquisition Act (1966) and own more than 80% of total land bank at present,[41] which makes for maintaining affordability of flats towards homeownership and asset building a possibility. Since the PAP came to power in 1959, it has contributed to the development of a stable political environment. The 'home-owning democracy' is one of the main tangible assets that has motivated citizens to support PAP and enhanced considerably the ruling party's legitimacy.[42] The government launched its ambitious housing programme in 1960 to meet the needs for decent homes while being ideologically motivated towards a creation of a more just and equal society.[43]

Third, as one of the effective roles of social connectivity, the third sector or self-governance organisations have played an important role towards asset building, especially to social asset building. These self-governance organisations acted as the bridge between government and HDB flat residents by providing feedback of residents' needs to let policy makers revise housing policies for better delivery of services.

Fourth, there is also the Confucianism-effect on homeownership to asset building. Singapore is a society with a majority of Chinese Singaporeans who are influenced greatly by Confucian values, emphasising the importance of home. From the point of Confucianism,

---

[40] Yong Chang Heo, "The development of housing policy in Singapore and the sources of path dependence", *Housing, Theory and Society*, *31*(4), pp. 429–446, 2014.

[41] Sock-Yong Phang, "Housing policy, wealth formation and the Singapore economy".

[42] Edwin Lee, *Singapore: The Unexpected Nation* (Singapore: Institute of Southeast Asian Studies, 2008); and Beng Huat Chua, "Navigating between limits: The future of public housing in Singapore".

[43] William S.W. Lim, "Assessment of Singapore's public housing programme and its relevance to other ASEAN primate cities", *IMPACT Magazine Philippines* and *Singapore Architectural Student Magazine*, pp. 1–9, 1972.

home is blended with the concept of family and house. Homeownership is closely associated with family, wealth and status.[44] Such social value is a precursor for the successful homeownership to asset building.

It is also necessary to acknowledge some drawbacks of homeownership to asset building while mainly focusing on the triumphant role in asset building in Singapore. First, homeownership creates housing stability, which will possibly result in less population mobility, in turn causing higher transportation costs and lower economic efficiency, as compared with the rental housing system. Rental housing market decreases transport demand by shortening the distance between residence and workplace, making the economy more efficient.[45] Moreover, homeownership assisted from CPF withdrawals may lead to a result of so-called 'asset rich but cash poor' society.[46] It is no exaggeration to say that every household tries to withdraw up to the maximum sum permitted out of its CPF account to pay for housing, not only to purchase the first flat but also to finance subsequent upgrading to a bigger flat.[47]

However, there is an uncertainty to financial asset building which may let the potential retirees holding HDB flats to get insufficient cash for pensions even though they can easily sell their apartments for financing. Actually, the elderly people have less motivation or preference to release their housing equity because this process is affected by a range of factors, including emotional and psychological attachment to the home as well as actual and symbolic financial security, anxieties about debt and the role of perceived personal and social stigma in

---

[44] James Lee, *Housing, Home ownership and social change in Hong Kong* (England: Ashgate, 1999).

[45] Chong-Yah Lim, *Policy options for the Singapore economy* (Singapore: McGraw-Hill, 1988).

[46] David McCarthy, Olivia S. Mitchell and John Piggott, "Asset rich and cash poor: Retirement provision and housing policy in Singapore", *Journal of Pension Economics & Finance* 1(3), pp. 197–222, 2002.

[47] Beng Huat Chua, "Navigating between limits: The future of public housing in Singapore".

shaping how older owners feel about equity release.[48] This means that there are some lease-owners who cannot get enough pensions by selling their HDB flats held in the past several decades. Kim-Lian Lim[49] projects that 60–70% of the 50–55-year-old cohort will not have sufficient funds to meet government stipulated minimums for retirement. Therefore, CPF accumulation, a social security system for financing pension, might deviate from its original objective due to excessive withdrawal for homeownership.

Many statistics show that the largest percentage of CPF expenditure was for housing programmes, which reduced the marginal efficiency of resources usage caused by over-allocation to the construction sector. The mechanism towards bigger HDB flats required more CPF withdrawals, which let to home owners walking on a tightrope, just as Manuel Castells, Ban Lee Goh and Yin-Wang Kwok[50] reveal that any wage restraints and cuts in CPF contribution rates mean that homeownership would become a burden. Furthermore, the issue on how to tradeoff between housing appreciation and affordability needs to be addressed. Asset-based housing policy calls on sustainable appreciation in housing value, in the form of higher housing price, which is the distinct challenge to affordability for young potential HDB owners.[51] With the popularity of bigger HDB flats and upgrading to private homeownership, household mobility creates co-movements of prices in public and private housing submarkets in the long-run.[52] It is not easy

---

[48] Lorna Fox O'mahony and Louise Overton, "Asset-based welfare, equity release and the meaning of the owned home", *Housing Studies, 30*(3), pp. 1–21, 2015.

[49] Kim-Lian Lim, "Implications of Singapore's CPF scheme on consumption choices and retirement incomes", *Pacific Economic Review, 6*(3), pp. 361–382, 2001.

[50] Manuel Castells, Ban Lee Goh and Yin-Wang Kwok, "The *shek kip mei* syndrome: Economic development and public housing in Hong Kong and Singapore", *Geographical Review, 82*(2), p. 222, 1992.

[51] Chong-Yah Lim, *Policy options for the Singapore economy*; Beng Huat Chua, "Navigating between limits: The future of public housing in Singapore"; and Beng Huat Chua, "Financialising public housing as an asset for retirement in Singapore".

[52] Tien-Foo Sing, I-Chun Tsai and Ming-Chi Chen, "Price dynamics in public and private housing markets in Singapore", *Journal of Housing Economics, 15*(4), pp. 305–320, 2006.

to increase the accessibility to public housing for the vulnerable group to support them on asset building. Some casual or part-time workers and some categories of contract workers are not covered by the CPF[53] thus having less opportunity to participate in asset building.

There are also some low-income families who have encountered or faced financial setback, prompting them to sell their HDB apartment. Rapid housing price appreciation can contribute to greater inequality in wealth distribution between various groups of winners and losers.[54] The government currently helps those who own to own more, and it deters those without from owning anything.[55] Housing affordability and appreciation may be the prisoner's dilemma. In addition, how to deal with the negative influences of financial crisis on asset building by homeownership is a difficult issue that has to be faced forever. As housing prices depreciated in financial crises of 1997 and 2007, it became evident that property was no longer reliable as a basis for welfare and economic security.[56]

Singapore is a small state which can be influenced easily by the global economic situation and this can be very volatile if the country does not have sufficient national reserves. Such reserves can only buffer for a non-prolonged period of economic recession. Once economic recession hits Singapore, public housing programme as an asset-building provision will come under pressure. The housing premium will not appreciate and it can take a slower down swing or become stuck in a rut. The 1997 economic downturn hit housing demand in Singapore hard,[57] which reveals that there are uncertainty

[53] Mukul G. Asher, *Compulsory savings in Singapore: An alternative to the welfare state.*

[54] Sock-Yong Phang, *Public housing — Appreciating assets?*, Working Paper, 1397, pp. 1–7, 2012.

[55] Sue Regan, "Asset-based welfare: Tackling poverty and inequality", *Public Policy Research*, 8(2), pp. 118–120, 2010.

[56] Richard Ronald, "Comparing homeowner societies: Can we construct an East–West model?", *Housing Studies*, 22(4), pp. 473–493, 2007.

[57] Richard Ronald and John Doling, "Shifting East Asian approaches to home ownership and the housing welfare pillar".

and limitation on homeownership to financial asset building. Indeed, as much as the CPF and HDB contributed to stability they were also accountable for speculative bubbles and the inability of the system to adjust to changing socioeconomic conditions.[58] Speculative behaviour and excessive investments in housing can lead to property bubbles, which when burst, can have serious consequences for the health of the financial sector and the economy.[59]

The advantages and disadvantages of homeownership to asset building in Singapore show that a deeper investigation on asset-based welfare policy should be considered. The future for asset-based welfare policy is perhaps uncertain and any answer is bound to be tentative.[60] The current state of asset policies is the beginning and not the end of debates.[61] Asset-based welfare policy is the hybrid of neo-liberalism and interventionism, having the obvious feature of the Third Way ideology. On the one hand, as per the character of neo-liberalism, asset-based welfare policy encourages welfare users to enhance autonomy and responsibility within individuals for their own financial future.[62] On the other hand, with regard to the features of interventionism, asset-based welfare policy, far from withdrawing the

---

[58] Beng Huat Chua, "Maintaining housing values under the condition of universal home ownership", *Housing Studies, 18*(5), pp. 765–780, 2003.

[59] Sock-Yong Phang, *Public housing — Appreciating assets?.*

[60] Alan Finlayson, "Financialisation, financial literacy and asset-based welfare", *The British Journal of Politics & International Relations, 11*(3), pp. 400–421, 2009.

[61] Rajiv Prabhakar, "The assets agenda and social policy", *Social Policy & Administration, 43*(1), pp. 54–69, 2009.

[62] Jane Newman and Elizabeth Vidler, "Discriminating customers, responsible patients, empowered users: Consumerism and the modernisation of health care", *Journal of Social Policy, 35*(2), pp. 193–209, 2006; Anthony Giddens, *The Third Way* (Cambridge, England: Polity, 1998); Jane Lewis and Rebecca Surender, *Welfare state change: Towards a Third Way* (Oxford, England: Oxford University Press, 2004); Matthew Watson, "Planning for a future of asset-based welfare? New labour, financialized economic agency and the housing market", *Planning Practice & Research, 24*(1), pp. 41–56, 2009; Nikolas Rose and Peter Miller, "Political power beyond the state: Problematics of government", *British Journal of Sociology, 43*(2), pp. 173–205,

state's intervention from social life, has gone to become deeper and stronger regulation and intervention in individual lives.[63]

Since neither neo-liberalism nor interventionism can cure all social problems independently, asset-based welfare policy also has no capability to solve all social diseases by itself. Under the asset-based welfare policy, a new contradiction is sharpening. Asset-based welfare policy contributes to the development of private property, a most effective guardian angel to freedom in the neo-liberalism context. However, for the sake of social benefit, government intervention has been placed to the extent that may limit and be a menace to liberty. Therefore, people's action to resist the power of state will be impeded in the name of acquiring choices for homeownership. If asset, or private property is not the guardian of freedom anymore, then the *raison d'etre* for the existence of assets itself has to be questioned extensively. Consequently, a roadmap should be developed where the basic social equality can be protected while guaranteeing asset or private property as the means of basic human right. The realisation of these two goals does not depend on how to implement law and institution, but relies on the ideology of implementing for law and institution. The asset-based welfare policy is an ex-ante preventative measure for refashioning welfare state but not destroying it. However, income policies and public services are ex-post curative policies for the continuing need. The relationship among asset, income benefits and public services should be complementary rather than a zero-sum one.[64]

1992; and Nikolas Rose, *Powers of freedom: Reframing political thought* (Cambridge, England: Cambridge University Press, 1999).

[63] Alan Finlayson, "Financialisation, financial literacy and asset-based welfare"; Rajiv Prabhakar, "The assets agenda and social policy"; and Richard Ronald and John Doling, "Shifting East Asian approaches to home ownership and the housing welfare pillar".

[64] Will Paxton, *Equal shares? Building a progressive and coherent asset-based welfare policy* (London, England: Institute for Public Policy Research, 2003); and Ruth Lister, "Poverty, material insecurity, and income vulnerability: The role of savings", in Sonia Sodha and Ruth Lister (eds.), *The saving gateway: From principles to practice* (London, England: Institute for Public Policy Research, 2006).

Appendix

Table 5A.1. Census of population 1980

Type of house	Total	One-person	Other no family nucleus	One family nucleus			Two family nucleus			More than two family nucleus
				Total	Married couple with a parent	Others	Total	Parents and children couples	Others	
(a) Private households by type of house and type of household										
Total	509,524	42,386	18,492	397,125	32,396	364,729	45,979	24,579	21,400	5,542
Detached bungalows	11,291	979	460	8,224	653	7,571	1,282	726	556	346
Semi-detached bungalows	12,466	685	405	9,869	879	8,990	1,316	728	588	191
Terrace houses	23,562	2,215	1,089	17,223	1,771	15,452	2,647	1,356	1,291	388
HDB and JTC flats	333,085	12,628	8,311	282,674	22,139	260,535	27,976	15,175	12,801	1,496
1-room	61,737	5,768	3,092	51,781	2,247	49,534	1,082	419	663	14
2-room	43,965	855	690	40,304	2,351	37,953	2,060	927	1,133	56
3-room	157,954	4,444	3,301	134,219	12,139	122,080	15,356	8,259	7,097	634
4-room	46,744	519	459	38,023	3,738	34,285	7,136	4,285	2,851	607
5-room	16,653	190	148	14,323	1,305	13,018	1,844	1,050	794	148
Other designs	6,032	852	621	4,024	359	3,665	498	235	263	37
Other public flats	10,398	1,386	426	8,116	458	7,658	449	234	215	21
Private flats	18,122	3,704	1,336	12,038	679	11,359	924	459	465	120
Shophouses	28,259	10,585	2,774	12,884	996	11,888	1,721	759	962	295
Attap/Zinc-roofed houses	62,864	5,729	2,413	42,623	4,691	37,932	9,437	5,034	4,403	2,662
Other types	9,477	4,475	1,278	3,474	130	3,344	227	108	119	23

(Continued)

Table 5A.1. (*Continued*)

Type of house	Total	Number of persons per household											Mean size
		1	2	3	4	5	6	7	8	9	10	11 or more	
(b) Private households by type of house and size of household													
Total	509,524	42,386	51,575	71,708	97,724	83,620	60,382	40,061	25,589	15,165	9,212	12,102	4.71
Detached bungalows	11,291	979	1,379	1,529	2,227	1,824	1,199	728	478	298	210	440	4.70
Semi-detached bungalows	12,466	685	1,119	1,609	2,947	2,455	1,518	932	491	293	163	254	4.72
Terrace houses	23,562	2,215	2,353	3,140	4,654	4,137	2,861	1,698	1,025	594	380	505	4.61
HDB and JTC flats	333,085	12,628	31,962	50,988	71,602	60,812	42,377	27,106	16,447	9,230	5,116	4,817	4.76
1-room	61,737	5,768	11,211	11,989	13,701	9,697	5,155	2,437	1,053	417	200	109	3.74
2-room	43,965	855	4,939	8,299	9,655	7,708	5,428	3,295	1,950	964	501	371	4.60
3-room	157,954	4,444	10,540	20,936	34,001	31,763	22,792	14,871	8,792	4,836	2,638	2,341	5.01
4-room	46,744	519	2,935	6,056	9,144	7,801	6,437	4,895	3,568	2,390	1,414	1,585	5.48
5-room	16,653	190	1,623	2,910	4,208	3,006	1,877	1,112	727	438	263	299	4.75
Other designs	6,032	852	714	798	893	837	688	496	357	185	100	112	4.46
Other public flats	10,398	1,386	1,408	1,921	2,292	1,488	884	449	292	123	77	78	3.86
Private flats	18,122	3,704	3,289	2,812	3,324	2,064	1,276	706	422	204	153	168	3.52
Shophouses	28,259	10,585	4,016	2,963	2,756	2,377	1,904	1,341	887	527	321	582	3.32
Attap/Zinc-roofed houses	62,864	5,729	5,162	5,909	7,101	7,799	7,807	6,695	5,298	3,711	2,681	4,972	5.77
Other types	9,477	4,475	887	837	821	664	556	406	249	185	111	286	3.31

(*Continued*)

Table 5A.1. (*Continued*)

(c) Private households by type of house and highest qualification of head

Type of house	Total	Full-time students	No qualification	Primary	Secondary	Upper secondary	Tertiary
Total	509,524	611	208,307	207,139	45,197	27,003	21,267
Detached bungalows	11,291	32	1,951	2,568	1,815	1,695	3,230
Semi-detached bungalows	12,466	45	1,612	3,155	2,378	2,217	3,059
Terrace houses	23,562	77	5,705	8,144	3,989	2,890	2,757
HDB and JTC flats	333,085	181	135,091	148,630	29,648	14,913	4,622
1–room	61,737	17	33,951	25,683	1,679	367	40
2–room	43,965	12	21,898	19,524	1,884	563	84
3–room	157,954	60	60,772	77,431	13,276	5,251	1,164
4–room	46,744	35	14,134	18,714	7,942	4,659	1,260
5–room	16,653	13	1,873	4,710	4,360	3,796	1,901
Other designs	6,032	44	2,463	2,568	507	277	173
Other public flats	10,398	5	1,608	2,921	2,051	1,664	2,149
Private flats	18,122	194	3,228	5,162	2,303	2,399	4,836
Shophouses	28,259	37	15,674	10,924	948	460	216
Attap/Zinc-roofed houses	62,864	27	38,896	21,463	1,668	630	180
Other types	9,477	13	4,542	4,172	397	135	218

(*Continued*)

Table 5A.1.   (*Continued*)

Type of house	Total	Number of persons in house													Mean number
		1	2	3	4	5	6	7	8	9	10	11–14	15–19	20 or more	
Total	467,142	16,620	45,170	66,823	93,018	80,201	58,065	38,847	25,130	15,246	9,681	12,931	3,526	1,884	5.14
(d) Census house by type of house and number of persons in house															
Detached bungalows	9,962	406	1,032	1,334	1,999	1,703	1,149	709	484	299	232	412	130	73	5.31
Semi-detached bungalows	12,114	430	1,056	1,569	2,898	2,441	1,521	934	502	302	175	247	31	8	4.86
Terrace houses	21,462	863	1,896	2,874	4,403	4,027	2,825	1,715	1,068	636	427	567	108	53	5.06
HDB and JTC flats	327,134	6,334	31,585	50,679	71,447	60,967	42,706	27,385	16,649	9,327	5,178	4,653	223	1	4.85
1-room	60,144	3,277	11,678	12,230	13,861	9,716	5,156	2,443	1,055	418	200	107	3	—	3.84
2-room	43,862	728	4,951	8,299	9,650	7,711	5,431	3,298	1,956	965	501	363	9	—	4.61
3-room	154,594	1,359	9,928	20,563	33,835	31,911	23,051	15,066	8,940	4,892	2,675	2,281	93	—	5.12
4-room	46,257	289	2,745	5,932	9,036	7,778	6,489	4,939	3,601	2,415	1,431	1,513	89	—	5.54
5-room	16,525	131	1,580	2,864	4,166	3,009	1,889	1,141	735	444	266	278	22	—	4.79
Other designs	5,752	550	703	791	899	842	690	498	362	193	105	111	7	1	4.67
Other public flats	10,064	879	1,548	1,923	2,295	1,493	888	452	296	129	78	76	7	—	3.99
Private flats	16,321	2,088	2,938	2,731	3,267	2,078	1,331	765	462	247	177	188	40	9	3.91
Shophouses	13,453	1,230	1,204	1,260	1,395	1,476	1,314	1,134	878	654	550	1,262	600	496	6.98
Attap/Zinc-roofed houses	50,313	2,921	3,169	3,723	4,543	5,372	5,782	5,337	4,540	3,456	2,739	5,327	2,280	1,124	7.21
Other types	6,319	1,469	742	730	771	644	549	416	251	196	125	199	107	120	4.97

(*Continued*)

Table 5A.1. (*Continued*)

(e) Census houses by type of house and number of households in house

Type of house	Total	Number of persons in house				Mean households
		1	2	3	4 or more	
Total	467,142	448,274	10,673	3,651	4,544	1.09
Detached bungalows	9,962	9,326	433	90	113	1.13
Semi-detached bungalows	12,114	11,913	141	30	30	1.03
Terrace houses	21,462	20,508	581	180	193	1.10
HDB and JTC flats	327,134	323,718	2,361	429	626	1.02
1–room	60,144	59,139	609	236	160	1.03
2–room	43,862	43,783	61	14	4	1.00
3–room	154,594	152,949	1,106	119	420	1.02
4–room	46,257	45,848	367	28	14	1.01
5–room	16,525	16,411	108	3	3	1.01
Other designs	5,752	5,588	110	29	25	1.05
Other public flats	10,064	9,828	188	20	28	1.03
Private flats	16,321	15,432	510	204	175	1.11
Shophouses	13,453	8,828	1,768	980	1,877	2.10
Attap/Zinc-roofed houses	50,313	43,127	4,375	1,600	1,211	1.25
Other types	6,319	5,594	316	118	291	1.50

Table 5A.2. Dwelling units under management

HDB Town		1-Room	2-Room*	3-Room	4-Room	5-Room	Exec	SA	Total
				Sold flats					
1	Ang Mo Kio	0	651	24,224	13,681	5,654	490	281	44,981
2	Bedok	0	875	22,633	20,398	10,390	2,714	234	57,244
3	Bishan	0	5	2,357	9,359	5,716	1,660	171	19,268
4	Bukit Batok	0	3	10,277	13,851	4,833	2,732	177	31,873
5	Bukit Merah	255	1,178	15,801	15,369	9,477	44	469	42,593
6	Bukit Panjang	0	465	3,678	16,699	10,425	3,381	380	35,028
7	Choa Chu Kang	0	365	2,137	22,485	15,293	4,762	515	45,557
8	Clementi	0	249	11,937	8,593	2,915	619	0	24,313
9	Geylang	0	816	11,233	9,607	3,591	830	239	26,316
10	Hougang	0	293	10,290	25,238	10,844	4,310	365	51,340
11	Jurong East	0	308	6,983	8,188	5,925	1,871	137	23,412
12	Jurong West	0	563	11,961	28,457	21,569	6,507	639	69,696
13	Kallang/Whampoa	0	506	13,313	10,178	5,392	504	38	29,931
14	Pasir Ris	0	282	490	11,641	9,379	7,460	181	29,433
15	Punggol	0	950	3,639	19,631	14,612	1,126	456	40,414
16	Queenstown	0	1,547	14,161	8,794	3,972	354	353	29,181
17	Sembawang	0	397	349	8,447	7,556	2,870	0	19,619

18	Sengkang	0	1,088	3,341	29,405	23,134	4,462	541	61,971
19	Serangoon	0	77	4,543	10,231	3,753	2,365	0	20,969
20	Tampines	0	353	13,093	28,631	17,312	5,846	649	65,884
21	Toa Payoh	0	759	15,096	9,756	6,017	854	300	32,782
22	Woodlands	0	433	6,343	27,763	19,639	6,191	855	61,224
23	Yishun	0	476	14,515	28,155	9,169	2,741	705	55,761
Other Estates									
24	Central Area	0	345	4,687	3,515	903	9	0	9,459
25	Bukit Timah	0	35	441	920	682	380	97	2,555
26	Marine Parade	0	26	3,036	1,798	1,677	0	0	6,537
Total		255	13,045	230,558	390,790	229,829	65,082	7,782	937,341

Note: *Includes 2-Room Flexi Flats.

(*Continued*)

Table 5A.2.   (*Continued*)

HDB Town		1-Room	2-Room	Rental 3-Room	4-Room	Total
1	Ang Mo Kio	1,318	2,855	13	1	4,187
2	Bedok	2,530	1,411	6	0	3,947
3	Bishan	396	0	0	0	396
4	Bukit Batok	385	239	1	0	625
5	Bukit Merah	4,476	4,599	164	0	9,239
6	Bukit Panjang	223	74	0	0	297
7	Choa Chu Kang	355	513	0	0	868
8	Clementi	474	467	10	0	951
9	Geylang	1,044	2,398	472	0	3,914
10	Hougang	532	624	28	0	1,184
11	Jurong East	352	110	23	0	485
12	Jurong West	540	1,169	698	0	2,407
13	Kallang/Whampoa	4,401	2,024	8	0	6,433
14	Pasir Ris	176	44	1	0	221
15	Punggol	871	462	0	0	1,333
16	Queenstown	575	1,699	49	0	2,323
17	Sembawang	321	371	0	0	692
18	Sengkang	685	391	0	0	1,076

19	Serangoon	272	247	0	0	519
20	Tampines	775	387	14	0	1,176
21	Toa Payoh	1,168	2,895	26	0	4,089
22	Woodlands	1,603	851	5	96	2,555
23	Yishun	1,038	724	15	0	1,777
Other Estates						
24	Central Area	2,075	971	52	14	3,112
25	Bukit Timah	0	0	0	0	0
26	Marine Parade	0	1,324	1	0	1,325
Total		26,585	26,849	1,586	111	55,131

(Continued)

Table 5A.2.   (*Continued*)

HDB Town	Sold flats Total	Rental Total	Total dwelling units	Dwelling units under construction	Dwelling units (DBSS) under construction	Dwelling units completed FY 2015/2016	Dwelling units completed (DBSS) FY 2015/2016
1 Ang Mo Kio	44,981	4,187	49,168	1,571	0	0	0
2 Bedok	57,244	3,947	61,191	1,058	0	1,104	0
3 Bishan	19,268	396	19,664	408	0	0	0
4 Bukit Batok	31,873	625	32,498	10,494	0	224	0
5 Bukit Merah	42,593	9,239	51,832	3,282	0	340	0
6 Bukit Panjang	35,028	297	35,325	0	0	862	0
7 Choa Chu Kang	45,557	868	46,425	2,602	0	4,032	0
8 Clementi	24,313	951	25,264	1,849	0	0	0
9 Geylang	26,316	3,914	30,230	1,334	0	975	0
10 Hougang	51,340	1,184	52,524	4,039	0	878	0
11 Jurong East	23,412	485	23,897	225	0	518	0
12 Jurong West	69,696	2,407	72,103	3,770	0	348	0
13 Kallang/Whampoa	29,931	6,433	36,364	3,565	0	626	0
14 Pasir Ris	29,433	221	29,654	0	0	0	447
15 Punggol	40,414	1,333	41,747	12,279	0	6,232	0
16 Queenstown	29,181	2,323	31,504	4,887	0	960	0
17 Sembawang	19,619	692	20,311	7,888	0	0	0

18	Sengkang	61,971	1,076	63,047	5,229	0	3,550	0
19	Serangoon	20,969	519	21,488	150	0	195	0
20	Tampines	65,884	1,176	67,060	4,913	0	462	0
21	Toa Payoh	32,782	4,089	36,871	3,703	0	436	0
22	Woodlands	61,224	2,555	63,779	6,265	0	1,002	0
23	Yishun	55,761	1,777	57,538	6,796	0	840	0
Other Estates								
24	Central Area	9,459	3,112	12,571	0	0	0	0
25	Bukit Timah	2,555	0	2,555	0	0	132	0
26	Marine Parade	6,537	1,325	7,862	0	0	0	0
Total		937,341	55,131	992,472	86,307	0	23,716	447

Chapter 6

Asset-Building Challenges with Low-Income Families

Irene Y.H. Ng

Introduction

What comes to mind when we say "assets"? To a typical individual in Singapore, this would include housing, savings, financial investments, and other 'store of value' that will grow through time, e.g., collectibles or antique. Michael Sherraden[1] calls these "tangible assets", and lists them as including (i) money savings; (ii) stocks, bonds, and other financial securities; (iii) real property; (iv) hard assets other than real estate, such as automobiles, jewelry, art and collectibles; (v) machines, equipment, tools, and other tangible components of production; (vi) durable household goods; (vii) natural resources; and (viii) copyrights, patents, and other intellectual property.

---

[1] Michael Sherraden, *Assets and the poor: A new American welfare policy* (New York: M.E. Sharpe, 1991).

What about to a low-income household? What would assets be? Yunju Nam, Jin Huang and Michael Sherraden[2] suggest that the asset holdings of low-income households are different from those of higher-income households. For low-income households, assets are often possessions that can be used for income generation (e.g., a motorbike, van or oven) or that can be converted to cash in financial emergencies (e.g., consumer durables such as furniture and household appliances). These assets depreciate rather than appreciate in value.

The aforementioned conceptualisations of assets reveal the disparity between asset holdings of poor and non-poor households. The typical assets of non-poor households grow in value, not so for poor households. This inequality provides the motivation for this chapter, to discuss the asset-building challenges faced by low-income families, and analyse the policy needs in addressing the gaps and challenges. The chapter will focus on two types of assets: housing and savings. It will also spend some time discussing household debt of low-income families. Debt can be viewed as negative assets. It shows the challenge of not only building the assets, but also the possible negative consequences of building the assets.

Beyond tangible assets, we could also look at other forms of assets that help low-income families improve their livelihoods. Examples include one's human capital, nested in education or health; or one's social networks. However, this chapter will not discuss these other types of assets. It will focus on the two basic assets of savings and housing, which have also been important policy focus in Singapore. Inequality in access to assets suggests the necessity of social policy to enable asset accumulation by households. In this respect, Singapore scores better than many other countries on several fronts. Our strong stance towards asset accumulation is clear through our homeownership and mandatory savings policies. However, the favourable statistics on the surface conceals challenges

---

[2] Yunju Nam, Jin Huang and Michael Sherraden, "Asset definitions", in Signe-Mary McKernan and Michael Sherraden (eds.), *Asset building and low-income families* (pp. 1–32) (Washington, D.C.: The Urban Institute Press, 2008).

especially for groups such as low-income families, which this chapter will discuss.

Housing

Nowhere else in the world has housing asset been as successfully promoted as in Singapore. At 90.9%,[3] Singapore has the highest homeownership rate in the world. Further, 79% of households live in public housing.[4] Such high rates are due to a housing policy that is focused on homeownership, "to encourage a property-owning democracy in Singapore and to enable Singapore citizens in the lower middle-income group to own their own homes."[5] Thus, unlike in other countries, where public housing is often synonymous to low-cost and low-quality housing for low-income households, public housing is almost a form of universal provision in Singapore.

Several factors helped to achieve such high rates of homeownership. First, through the Land Acquisition Act 1966, the government has the right to acquire land for public projects at below market price, thus reducing costs. Second, high progressive subsidies are given to first-time buyers at preferential housing loan rates. Third, compulsory saving contributions to the Central Provident Fund (CPF) are allowed for housing purchases. The use of CPF savings for home purchase has been the most instrumental in unlocking the door to homeownership.[6] Today, many people 'empty out' the Ordinary Account in their

[3] Department of Statistics Singapore, *Home ownership rate of resident households* (Singapore: The Author, 2017). Retrieved on 5 July 2017 from http://www.singstat.gov.sg/statistics/visualising-data/charts/home-ownership-rate-of-resident-households

[4] Department of Statistics Singapore, *Resident households by tenancy* (Singapore: The Author, 2017). Retrieved on 5 July 2017 from http://www.tablebuilder.singstat.gov.sg/publicfacing/createDataTable.action?refId=851

[5] Housing and Development Board (HDB), 1964, Cited in Sook Yee Tan, *Private ownership of public housing in Singapore* (Singapore: Times Academic Press, 1998), p. 13.

[6] Yong Chang Heo, "The development of housing policy in Singapore and the sources of path dependence", *Housing, Theory and Society*, 31(4), pp. 429–446, 2014; and Beng Huat Chua, "Navigating between limits: The future of public housing in Singapore", *Housing Studies*, 29(4), pp. 520–533, 2014.

CPF savings to purchase their flat, to the extent that the saying "asset rich, but cash poor" has become ubiquitous.

At 90.9% homeownership rate, this means that even low-income households have been able to own homes. Only for the lowest-income households who cannot afford to own, is there the Public Rental Scheme. From Poh Leng Teo's observation, "[c]onsidered as a final social safety net for the very poor, the rent for these HDB flats has been kept low, ranging from SGD26 to SGD240 per month for a one-room flat depending on the family's income level."[7] Although most families in public rental flats stay there for years, the message is that subsidised rental flats are meant to be temporary shelters through two yearly reviews of tenancy. The eventual aim is towards home ownership.[8]

The emphasis on homeownership for low-income households can be seen from a factsheet by the Housing and Development Board (HDB) showing how a family with a monthly income of S$1,000 can afford the smallest flat type of two-room flexi. Conditions are strict. The factsheet prices a new two-room flexi flat in a non-mature estate at S$110,000. This is more than eight times the annual income of a S$1,000[9] per month household, which is S$12,000. However, with government grants of up to S$80,000 if the applicant is a first-time buyer, the remaining amount that the applicant needs to pay is only S$30,000, 2.5 times the low-income family's annual income. The family will need to pay only S$161 a month for a 20-year loan, or

---

[7] Poh Leng Teo, *Experiences of homeless families on the interim rental housing scheme in Singapore*, Unpublished doctoral dissertation, National University of Singapore, Singapore, 2015.

[8] Housing and Development Board, "How is HDB helping low-income households with a roof over their head?", *Online Buzz*, 2013. Retrieved on 6 July 2017 from http://www.hdbspeaks.sg/fi10/fi10336p.nsf/cw/SuspendHigherTierRents?Open Document; and Housing and Development Board, "Why can't HDB provide rental flats for all?", *Housing Speaks*, 2014. Retrieved on 6 July 2017 from http://www.hdbspeaks.sg/fi10/fi10336p.nsf/cc/PublicRentalFlats

[9] The HDB factsheet assumes that the S$1,000 includes CPF contributions of both employer and employee.

S$139 a month for a 25-year loan. These monthly mortgage payments can be paid from the CPF.[10]

Thus, with the sizeable grants, most low-income families in Singapore can indeed afford homeownership. A family income of S$1,000 a month is below the S$1,900 household income criterion for government financial assistance. Ironically, then, even families who need financial assistance can afford to purchase a home. Perhaps this irony is one of the beauty of Singapore's homeownership policy, that the basic need of a shelter is taken care of even for families who cannot afford daily expenses.

However, the picture is not so rosy. The aforementioned scenario where the family pays from the CPF a mortgage of S$161 or S$139 a month depends on strong assumptions. The first assumption is that the earning person pays CPF in the first place. Many low-waged workers are in casual jobs that pay no CPF. One obvious reason is that low-income families need liquidity to meet present expense needs. Between a permanent position with lower take-home salary and CPF, and a daily waged or contract position with higher take-home pay but no CPF, some choose the latter. Examples of such jobs include gig economy occupations such as delivery, and contract-by-contract cleaning work.

Another assumption that might not hold relates to the measurement of housing affordability. Common metrics of housing affordability include three times one's annual income and monthly payments of 30% of one's monthly income. However, these metrics might be unrealistic for low-income families, when they already struggle to meet expenses on daily necessities. In Singapore, because the monthly mortgage is likely taken from CPF, the purchasing power problem is not immediately apparent. However, "asset rich, cash poor" then becomes worse for low-income families. Retirement adequacy of CPF has been questioned, especially for low-income families who have little or no alternative sources of savings (see next section). Thus, the

---

[10] Housing and Development Board, "How can I own a BTO flat with a monthly income of $1,000?", *Housing Speaks*, 2015. Retrieved on 6 July 2017 from http://www.hdbspeaks.sg/fi10/fi10336p.nsf/cc/OwnaBTOFlatwith1000aMonth?OpenDocument

threshold for what is affordable housing might need to be lower for low-income households.

To address the problem of retirement inadequacy for lower-income individuals who are "asset rich, cash poor", initiatives such as the Lease Buyback Scheme (LBS) and two-room Flexi Scheme were introduced. The former allows those who are 64 years old and older, and had bought four-room flats or below, to sell part of the house lease back to HDB while continuing to stay in the house.[11] The latter scheme enables elderly who are 55 years old and above to sell their house in exchange for new two-rooms studio apartments with shorter leases that are often in non-mature estates (and therefore cheaper).[12] This gives the elderly person cash for the twilight years and a roof over one's head.

The aforementioned discussion throws light on a fact brought up in the introduction earlier, that for low-income families, housing as an asset serves more of a last resort buffer to be sold, and not as a store of value that appreciates as is the case for flats of higher-income families. A low-income family that can afford to buy a two-room flat with S$80,000 worth of grants can enjoy the monetary gains of selling the flat only if it can afford to buy another flat. However, with working-class wage stagnation experienced in the past decades,[13] this is a tall order for many low-income families. A two-room flexi flat also does not appreciate in value as much as bigger flats. A higher income couple who purchases a five-room BTO for S$400,000 can expect capital gains of as much as S$200,000 at the end of the minimum occupation period of five years. With higher incomes as they work longer, the capital gains from the subsidised flat can propel them towards private

---

[11] Housing and Development Board, "Lease buyback scheme", 2015. Retrieved on 5 July 2017 from http://www.hdb.gov.sg/cs/infoweb/residential/living-in-an-hdb-flat/for-our-seniors/lease-buyback-scheme

[12] Housing and Development Board, "2-room flexi flats", 2015. Retrieved on 5 July 2017 from http://www.hdb.gov.sg/cs/infoweb/residential/buying-a-flat/new/2room-flexi-flats

[13] Irene Y.H. Ng, Yi Ying Ng and Poh Choo Lee, "After wage restructuring: A case study of cleaning job conditions in Singapore", *The Economics and Labour Relations Review* (forthcoming).

homeownership for additional capital gains or reap the gains monetarily by downsizing.

Furthermore, that a low-income family can afford to *purchase* a home does not mean that the family can actually afford to *live in* the home. Besides the monthly mortgage, there are other household related payments such as furnishings, utilities, and town council fees. A common reason for applications to the ComCare Short-to-Medium Term Assistance (CC SMTA) is the accumulation of debt that the family can no longer manage on their own. In our study of 832 beneficiaries of the Work Support Programme (WSP)[14] by the Ministry of Social and Family Development (MSF), my colleagues and I found that housing-related arrears were two of the top three reasons for applying for ComCare assistance: 42% said it is because they chalked up too much mortgage or rental arrears, and 60% said it is because they had too much utilities arrears.[15] Often times, the arrears accumulated due to the loss or change of a job, the birth of a child, divorce, imprisonment, or a health episode such as a stroke or cancer that might also lead to job loss. Other times, it is simply because the low wages earned are insufficient to sustain the housing-related bills.[16]

The WSP research followed beneficiaries through five waves during the period 2010 to 2017. Figure 6.1 shows the house-related arrears rates among 327 beneficiaries who had answered our survey for all five waves. It shows that 39% had mortgage arrears, which halved to 19% by wave 5. This is still a substantial percentage. However, the most common type of arrears in wave 1 was for rent, where 76% had rent arrears. By wave 5, the percentage decreased to

---

[14] This programme was later expanded and renamed as ComCare Short-to-Medium Term Assistance.

[15] Irene Y.H. Ng, Alex Lee, Tee Liang Ngiam, Keng Weng Ho and Nesamani Tharmalingam, *Longitudinal study of families placed on longer term assistance under the Work Support Programme: Second Annual Report: January to December 2011,* Unpublished report submitted to the Ministry of Community Development Youth and Sports, National University of Singapore, Singapore, 2012.

[16] Ministry of Social and Family Development, *Approach in tackling homeless cases,* 2016. Retrieved from https://www.msf.gov.sg/media-room/Pages/Approach-in-tackling-homeless-cases.aspx

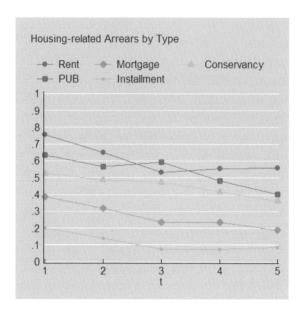

Figure 6.1. Housing-related arrears rates of WSP beneficiaries

56%, but this is still more than half the respondents. The other house-related arrears also displayed a similar trend: decreasing but substantial proportions of respondents possessed each type of arrears.

That 39% owed mortgage arrears and 76% owed rent arrears means that 37% owed both types of arrears in wave 1. Indeed in our five waves' analysis, 12.5% ever transited from homeownership to rental, and 14% from rental to homeownership. Again, this throws light on the fact that there are significant numbers of low-income families who had purchased flats, but could not upkeep them, even as housing aspiration pushed some rental dwellers towards homeownership.

Figure 6.2 shows the arrears amounts owed of each type of arrears. Naturally, mortgage arrears values are the highest. The arrears amounts of the other types of arrears are lower, but still substantial. The values are also not declining. That is, although the proportion of respondents with each arrears type declined, for those who still had that arrears, the debt size was not decreasing.

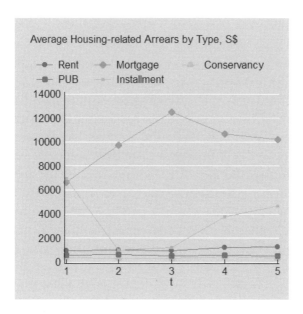

Figure 6.2. Housing-related arrears amounts of WSP beneficiaries

For every family on government assistance with housing-related arrears, there are certainly other low-income households that have managed without going into the red. There would also be those who do chalk up arrears but of smaller amounts or have other informal sources of help such that they do not apply for assistance. In total, the MSF reports helping 29,511 households in CC SMTA in 2015.[17] Many of these families have housing-related arrears.

The inability to keep up the payments for the purchased home came to light in 2007 when news reports of homeless families camping in parks started. It was found that many had owned homes, but sold without being able to buy another. Having enjoyed subsidies as first-time buyers previously, they no longer qualify for subsidies, and

[17] Ministry of Social and Family Development, *Community Care Endowment Fund: Annual Report for Financial Year 2015*, 2016. Retrieved from https://www.msf.gov. sg/media-room/Documents/ComCare%20Annual%20Report%20FY15.pdf

flats in the open market are too expensive.[18] This reflects the challenges of helping low-income second-timer families have access to housing asset. A growing group of homeowners could not sustain their homes for various reasons, e.g., purchasing too large a flat that was beyond the family's means; divorce; ill health leading to loss of employment and thus an inability to service the mortgage; selling the first flat for cash gain but not finding another etc. Between 2005 and 2015, MSF helped 300 homeless cases each year.

To better assist families with housing needs, the Interim Rental Housing Scheme (IRHS) was started in 2009.[19] The Fresh Start Housing Scheme (FSHS) was also started in 2016, to help the families in public rental have a second chance at homeownership. FSHS allows low-income families with children below 16 years old who had previously bought a flat before to purchase a two-room short lease flat (termed as two-room Flexi).[20] Families that are eligible for the FSHS must have occupied a rental flat for at least two years without accumulating three or more months of rental arrears in the preceding 12 months, and have at least one applicant in stable employment for the past 12 months. Average gross monthly household income cannot exceed S$6,000.[21] Applicants must also obtain a Letter of Social Assessment (LSA) from MSF, which assesses for family stability, employment stability, ability to manage their finances well, and regularity of school attendance for all children.[22] After collection of key,

---

[18] R. Basu, "Number of homeless people doubles; more than half found sleeping in void decks; most of those picked up are placed in homes", *The Sunday Times*, 31 January 2010; Bow Tan Mah, *Speech presented at the Committee of Supply Debate, 6 February 2009, Singapore* [Transcript]. Retrieved from http://www.mnd.gov.sg; Poh Leng Teo, *Experiences of homeless families on the interim rental housing scheme in Singapore*.

[19] Boon Wan Khaw, *Getting IRH to work better* [Blog message], 30 December 2011. Retrieved from https://mndsingapore.wordpress.com/2011/12/30/getting-irh-to-work-better/

[20] Housing and Development Board, "Fresh start housing scheme", 2016. Retrieved on 5 July 2017 from http://www.hdb.gov.sg/cs/infoweb/residential/buying-a-flat/new/schemes-and-grants/fresh-start-housing-scheme

[21] Housing and Development Board, "Fresh start housing scheme".

[22] Housing and Development Board, "Fresh start housing scheme".

the applicants are to undergo annual reviews by MSF to renew their LSA until five years after key collection.[23]

The proportion of rental dwellers who had been homeowners increased from 52% in 2010 to 59% in 2015 (Yeo, 2015). This and other types of families requiring housing security meant that more rental flats had to be built. The number of rental flats was targeted to increase from 50,000 in 2013 to 60,000 in 2017 (Chang, 2013). Still the government aims for the stock of public rental to be kept below 7% of all housing (Teo, 2016). Housing aspiration among public housing renters is also high. ~~Irene I.Y. Ng~~ Ng Kok Hoe (2017) found that 69% of the 1,075 rental flat respondents he surveyed aspired towards home-ownership. This is despite the difficulties of sustaining housing security, with more than half of Ng's respondents feeling worried about housing stability.

The aforementioned situations of needing to build more rental and two-room flats are in sharp contrast to the 1980s and 1990s, when the HDB stopped building smaller-sized flats, in the belief that as incomes rose, the need for smaller flats would disappear.[24] Alas, incomes especially of rank-and-file jobs did not rise. Instead, they stagnated or even declined in the 1990s to 2000s. Thus, the challenge of housing affordability is as much a problem of raising wages.

At the same time, flat prices kept rising. Housing price escalation was so acute in the 2000s that this quote from a letter to *The Straits Times* has often been repeated: "In 1981, I earned $800 plus as a fresh graduate. At that time, one of my colleagues bought a five-room HDB flat for $35,000. Now, a graduate's pay has risen about four times but HDB flat prices have risen more than 11 times."[25]

The aforementioned trends and the policy responses reveal the challenges of keeping the strong homeownership policy, especially with the escalation of housing prices that make housing less and less

---

[23] Housing and Development Board, "Fresh start housing scheme".

[24] Beng Huat Chua, "Navigating between limits: The future of public housing in Singapore".

[25] Cheryl Lee, "Housing affordability key to good parenting", *The Straits Times*, 25 October 2011.

affordable. In fact, the homeownership policy might have created an inflation bias because of the need to ensure housing price appreciation for a homeowning nation. In this sense, housing as an asset has displaced the purpose of housing as a public good.[26]

While much has been done to tamper the housing price escalation and wage stagnation experienced in the 2000s, the task is uphill. In a land scarce, small island nation with a policy philosophy of homeownership creating an inflation bias, and the structural problems in the labour market tending to drive wages apart, it will be more and more difficult to maintain homeownership affordability for low-income families.

The general analysis in this chapter has only scratched the surface of the housing challenge for low-income families. Most of the discussion so far applies mainly to low-income families with married or divorced couples. Low-income families are made of a diverse demographic pool. Word limit does not permit a lengthy discussion of various low-income family types that are generally excluded from the public housing market, such as singles, single parents, and transnational families. With housing affordable to normative families only through large government subsidies, the problem that the alternative family types experience is not homeownership, but mere affordability of having a shelter.

All in all, the success of 'housing a nation' hides or amplifies the challenges of helping low-income households acquire and maintain this important asset in Singapore. Homeownership might instead be a burden to low-income households, sinking them into a life of debt and hardship instead of a life of hope and aspiration that assets are supposed to bring.

Savings

In life cycle and buffer stock theories, savings acts as consumption smoothing and a buffer for rainy days. When there is no income, for

---

[26] Beng Huat Chua, "Financialising public housing as an asset for retirement in Singapore", *International Journal of Housing Policy, 15*(1), pp. 27–42, 2015.

example due to retrenchment or retirement, savings can be drawn on to meet expenses. Can low-income households save? In their years of doing research on matched savings accounts for low-income families, Michael Sherraden and colleagues found that low-income families who are not the poorest of the poor can save. However, both structural and individual barriers need to be addressed, and often times, the structural facilitation (e.g., through automatic accounts set up for families) enhances individual motivation to save.[27]

In matched savings programmes for adults, called individual development accounts (IDAs), participants were encouraged to save towards goals that include homeownership, home maintenance and repairs, business ownership, education, and retirement. However, Michal Grinstein-Weiss and associates did not find long-term effects of matched savings on most of these outcomes except for education enrolment and home maintenance repairs.[28] Neither were effects on wealth or mental health found.[29] The authors concluded that a short-term program of three years might not be able to sustain long-term impacts, especially if there are structural factors preventing asset accumulation, factors such as low wages and pressing expense needs. Instead, savings programmes might be better targeted for incremental purposes such as home repairs rather than lumpy investments such as a home.

Sherraden and colleagues found greater effectiveness with child development accounts (CDAs), especially when the accounts are

[27] Yunju Nam, Jin Huang and Michael Sherraden, "Asset definitions"; and Sondra G. Beverly, Michael Sherraden, Reid Cramer, Trina R. Williams Shanks, Yunju Nam and Min Zhan, "Determinants of asset holdings", in Signe-Marie McKernan and Michael Sherraden (eds.), *Asset building and low-income families* (pp. 89–151) (Washington, D.C.: Urban Institute, 2008).

[28] Michal Grinstein-Weiss, Michael Sherraden, William G. Gale, William M. Rohe, Mark Schreiner and Clinton Key, "Long-term impacts of Individual Development Accounts on homeownership among baseline renters: Follow-up evidence from a randomized experiment", *American Economic Journal: Economic Policy*, 5(1), pp. 122–145, 2013.

[29] William M. Rohe, Clinton Key, Michal Grinstein-Weiss, Mark Schreiner and Michael Sherraden, "The impacts of Individual Development Accounts, assets, and debt on future orientation and psychological depression", *Journal of Policy Practice*, 16(1), pp. 24–22, 2017.

given automatically and progressively, where poorer children were matched with greater amounts of savings.[30] The CDAs, set up automatically at birth with an initial deposit to save for college, increased the likelihood of saving, saving amounts, and parents' expectations for college. The effects were stronger for poorer children and were attributed to the automatic accounts and the initial deposit, which poor families would otherwise not have started. Progressivity also benefited disadvantaged children more, but the effect of automatic enrolment was more instrumental. Sherraden and colleagues conclude that such savings programmes are most beneficial when given as universal child accounts at the large-scale policy level, rather than as small targeted programs with conditions.

The aforementioned findings from a long-term set of studies on savings for the poor point to several important facts. First, while it is possible to help low-income families save, the implementation costs are high and effects unsustainable in light of structural barriers that prevent saving by low-income households beyond the initial subsidies. Second, poor families who struggle to meet daily expenses have difficulties saving. Third, universal monetary provision for long-term goals such as post-secondary education for children appear more important to generate the kind of asset accumulation and resulting benefits than programmes targeted towards individual efforts to save.

What do these findings mean for Singapore? Savings is clearly emphasised in national policy. Adults are mandated to save through the CPF. For children, the Baby Bonus Scheme gives a cash gift at birth, one-for-one matched savings through CDAs, and a First Step grant when the CDA is opened. As national universal policies, the CPF and Baby Bonus Scheme (at least the cash gift component) are at the levels that Sherraden and colleagues argue will reap the most benefits of savings. However, challenges abound in truly helping low-income families tap on these policy tools to accumulate assets, as the next few paragraphs will discuss.

---

[30] Sondra G. Beverly, Margaret M. Clancy and Michael Sherraden, *The early positive impacts of Child Development Accounts* (St. Louis, MO: Washington University, Center for Social Development, June 2016).

The CPF is automatic for all salaried Singaporeans and permanent residents. As much as 37% of their earned income goes into CPF. Table 6.1 reproduces the allocation rates of CPF monies. The largest share goes to the Ordinary Account, from which CPF members can withdraw for housing, investments and education purposes. The Special Account yields a higher interest rate and is earmarked only for retirement. The MediSave Account is for healthcare expenses, for payment of medical insurance premiums (MediShield and integrated plans), co-payments in hospitalisation and payments for certain outpatient treatments.

As shown in the previous section, the availability of CPF savings for housing purchase has enabled low-income households to access an important asset, a home. CPF also acts as an important buffer stock for many Singaporeans. It is an important source of retirement and healthcare expenses, arguably more so for low-income households who otherwise might set aside no or insufficient funds for these needs. With the government 'forcing' individuals to set aside such savings for healthcare and retirement, low-income families at least have CPF as buffer.

Table 6.1. CPF allocation rates from 1 January 2016 for private sector employees and public sector non-pensionable employees

| Employee's age (years) | Allocation rates from 1 January 2016 for monthly wages ≥ $750 | | |
	Ordinary Account (% of wage)	Special Account (% of wage)	MediSave Account (% of wage)
35 and below	23	6	8
36 to 45	21	7	9
46 to 50	19	8	10
51 to 55	15	11.5	10.5
56 to 60	12	3.5	10.5
61 to 65	3.5	2.5	10.5
Above 65	1	1	10.5

Source: From https://www.cpf.gov.sg/employers/employerguides/employer-guides/paying-cpf-contributions/cpf-contribution-and-allocation-rates

However, the adequacy of CPF savings for retirement and healthcare expenses has been questioned. One aspect is again the fact that large amounts of CPF savings are locked in housing. Weng Tat Hui[31] argues that retirement adequacy is at risk when housing purchase, housing price escalation (and thus larger amounts of CPF savings have to be used for housing), and unemployment are factored in. In fact, for lower-income households, their CPF funds are adequate for retirement only if "there are no withdrawals for housing or other investments" (p. 70). Ngee Choon Chia[32] also argues that "being a work-based system", CPF cannot ensure retirement adequacy for "low-wage workers with low CPF accumulation, those unable to work because of disabilities, stay-at-home mothers without CPF savings, and elderly without any familial support (p. 274).

Healthcare costs have also escalated. Although it is highly subsidised, with Singaporeans bearing as little as only 20% of a hospital bill for a Class C Ward (Ministry of Health, 2014), the 20% can still be unaffordable to some, especially if one's insurance coverage is limited. Although there is MediFund for those who are still unable to afford medical care, it is means-tested and therefore not all low-income families can qualify. There are also medical expenses which are not covered by MediSave or hospitalisation insurances, e.g., primary care or long-term post-acute care. Thus, besides "asset rich, cash poor", another saying is that one can afford to die, but not afford to fall sick in Singapore.

The aforementioned challenges undoubtedly affect low-income households more. Low-income families are also over-represented among those who do not contribute to CPF or do so only sporadically. These include contract and self-employed workers and homemakers. The latter group becomes a high-risk group in the event of

---

[31] Weng Tat Hui, "Retirement funding and adequacy", in Faizal Bin Yahya (ed.), *Inequality in Singapore* (Singapore: World Scientific, 2015).
[32] Ngee Choon Chia, "Adding a basic pillar to the Central Provident Fund System: An actuarial analysis", *The Singapore Economic Review*, 60(3), doi: 10.1142/S021759081550037X, 2015.

divorce. With 3.76 million CPF members and 1.79 million active members,[33] while 96% of the resident population of 3.93 million are CPF members, only 46% are active members.[34]

To address the aforementioned problems especially for elderly low-income Singaporeans, new schemes such as CPF Life (a form of annuity), Silver Support (a form of pension for elderly who had been poor their whole life), and MediShield Life (universal basic medical insurance) were introduced in the past few years. These point to the fact that despite a compulsory savings scheme at a high rate of 37% at the peak earning years, assets accumulated are still insufficient for many.

These suggest that universal forms of providing public goods such as housing, healthcare and old-age expenses are still necessary. Asset accumulation cannot replace the need for universal social protection. However, assets-based policies have been important in building a system where some individual responsibility is enforced through mandatory savings and designated uses of the savings. These in turn might ameliorate the large fiscal burden of universal programs.

Turning next to savings for children, the amounts given by the government under the Baby Bonus Scheme are generous. The cash gift amounts to S$8,000 for the first and second child, and S$10,000 for the third and subsequent child. The First Step grant gives S$3,000 as an initial deposit, and any additional amount saved by the parents will be matched by the government dollar-for-dollar up to a cap.[35] Parents can save for their children in the CDA until just before the child turns 13, and any remaining amounts will be transferred to a post-secondary education account (PSEA) where parents can continue to save and receive the dollar-for-dollar matching until the child

---

[33] Central Provident Fund, 2017.

[34] Department of Statistics, 2016.

[35] Ministry of Social and Family Development, *Baby Bonus Scheme frequently asked question*, 2017. Retrieved from http://www.ifaq.gov.sg/BBSS/apps/fcd_faqmain.aspx#FAQ_134031

is 18.[36] When the child turns 30, any unused amount in the PSEA will be transferred to their CPF account.[37]

The Baby Bonus website states that it meets two purposes: (i) to defray the costs of raising children; and (ii) to save for the educational and healthcare needs of children (Ministry of Social and Family Development, 2016). The CDA can be opened only with designated banks and be used with approved organisations. In a parliamentary reply in 2014, MSF revealed that 95% of children in cohorts 2006 to 2013 possess CDA, with 48% having saved up to the maximum co-savings cap. Of the latter, 10% fully used the CDA.[38] The reply does not provide information on the extent of savings or withdrawal of the other 52%, except that 85% of CDA funds are used on education and 15% on healthcare. While the 5% without CDA is low, there is no information on whether this 5% is over-represented by certain groups, e.g., lower-income families. MSF expects the percentage of children without CDAs to decrease, because families are given 12 years to save in the CDA. However, birth is the natural point for the opening of a CDA, and unless there are other time points in a child's life where CDAs are actively promoted, the 5% will likely not decrease much further.

Therefore, questions remain on the distributional access and use of CDA in terms of three factors: whether a family opens a CDA account, how much the family saves in the CDA, and how much and how quickly the family spends from the CDA. Anecdotal accounts from parents suggest that most of the CDA funds are drained in a few years due to high costs of childcare and pre-school. Anecdotal accounts of social workers and research by my colleagues and I also suggest that

---

[36] Ministry of Social and Family Development, *Baby Bonus Scheme frequently asked question.*

[37] Ministry of Education, *About the PSEA*, 2016. Retrieved from https://www.moe.gov.sg/education/post-secondary/post-secondary-education-account/about-the-psea

[38] Ministry of Social and Family Development, *Savings for Child Development Account*, 2014. Retrieved from https://www.msf.gov.sg/media-room/Pages/Savings-in-Child-Development-Account.aspx#; and Ministry of Social and Family Development, *Statistics of children without Child Development Account (CDA)*, 2014. Retrieved from https://www.msf.gov.sg/media-room/Pages/Statistics-of-children-without-Child-Development-Account-(CDA).aspx

many low-income families either do not register for or make deposits into the CDAs. In our study, among 138 respondents who have children younger than five years old, 77% said they have a savings account with their children, including Baby Bonus or CDA. The reported household savings was on average S$212.[39] There is likely substantial under-reporting by respondents. Still, given the generosity of Baby Bonus, the reported savings rates and amounts suggest that many of the low-income households surveyed did not open a CDA, made no or little deposits, or used up the Baby Bonus very quickly. Although registration for a CDA is easy through a simple online form, the need for registration instead of automatic enrolment probably still leads to some not doing so. The people who do not register are likely those who feel they do not have funds to deposit in the first place.

Thus, CPF and Baby Bonus, while offering low-income families basic income security, are regressive asset accumulation tools. The more one contributes to CPF or CDA, the more one yields in terms of the higher-than-market interest rates in CPF and matched savings in the CDA. This leads to an interesting irony that while CPF and CDA enable low-income families to possess the assets of a house or a savings account, they reinforce wealth inequality through regressivity in asset accumulation. Although progressivity is injected e.g., through rebates into CPF where smaller-sized HDB flats are given more, the main design on these policies are regressive. It also appears that while Baby Bonus and CDA are designed for longer-term human capital development, they have played largely the roles of allaying consumption needs of a child's initial years instead of long-term savings towards education. This was also the case for the CDAs studied by Sherraden and colleagues.

Debt and Living in Poverty

One goal of asset accumulation is to increase net worth, computed as the difference between assets and liabilities. Unfortunately, a family's

---

[39] Irene Y.H. Ng, Qi Yan Ong and Walter Theseira, *Debt relief: Short & medium run effects*, Unpublished manuscript, Social Service Research Centre, National University of Singapore, Singapore, 2017.

net worth might not increase even while they are building assets through housing grants and CPF. In fact, as shown in the previous section on housing, for some low-income families, housing-related debt becomes a burden of homeownership.

In our WSP research, my colleagues and I found that among 327 respondents who answered all five waves of the survey, 78% of respondents in the first wave had arrears. By the last wave, 52% still had arrears. Most of the arrears are in necessary goods, such as housing related bills. Arrears amounted to a mean of S$5,748 in the first wave and S$3,180 in the last wave. Although arrears amounts have decreased, they are still substantial and 1.8 times of the average household income of S$1,808 (Ng *et al.*, 2018). Thus, living with debt is common among low-income households, and the composition of the debts suggests that the debts are more to do with not earning enough for necessities than with overspending.

Research has also shown that anxiety over debt and finances takes a toll on one's cognitive and mental health. In the famous article by Anandi Mani, Sendhil Mullainathan, Eldar Shafir and Jiaying Zhao,[40] findings from two research studies show that poverty impedes cognitive function, rather than cognitive inferiority leading to poverty. The authors' laboratory experiments found that when induced with thoughts about finances, the cognitive performance of poor participants deteriorated, but not that of well-off participants. However, experiments are artificial. Thus, the authors also reported findings among Indian sugarcane farmers in natural settings. They "found that the same farmer shows diminished cognitive performance before harvest, when poor, as compared with after harvest, when rich" (p. 976).

Research in the local context also confirms the relationship between debt and mental health. In the WSP study, higher rates of generalised anxiety were found among respondents with more types of debt (Ng *et al.*, 2018). In our evaluation of a debt relief program, Qi Yan Ong, Walter Theseira and I found that anxiety rates decreased and cognitive functioning improved after the debt relief. The effects were sustained 12 months after debt relief. Qualitative interviews also

---

[40] Anandi Mani, Sendhil Mullainathan, Eldar Shafir and Jiaying Zhao, "Poverty impedes cognitive function", *Science*, *341*(6149), pp. 976–980, 2013.

support the anxiety inducing effects of debt. Interviewees talked about being so worried over finances that they could not sleep. Some were diagnosed for clinical depression. In Hillary Hui-Wen Hoo's study of eight low-income women with debt, the most common refrain when respondents were asked to summarize their experience of debt was "stress" and rumination over the debt situation, such that respondents talked about being tired of thinking.[41]

The aforementioned findings point to tremendous mental and cognitive strain from living in poverty and debt. Yet for low-income families, the margins of error and for deviation from tight budgets are very small. In their seminal book titled *Poor Economics*, Abhijit Banerjee and Esther Duflo describe how poor farmers and women are unable to save because of temptation goods such as tobacco and sweet teas.[42] Somehow these temptations become more desirous because they are things that non-poor people take for granted. If they exercise self-control and do not given in to the temptations, their lives can be improved, e.g., by purchasing fertiliser for higher production.

While it is easy for bystanders to say one solution lies in improving savings motivation, it is double-standard to expect such high extent of self-control when temptation goods to middle-class individuals are branded goods and luxury lifestyles which poor individuals often cannot even dream of. Furthermore, whereas the consequences to the middle class of giving in to a temptation or making a poor purchase decision might simply be a dent in one's bank account, one poor choice could be dire for low-income families.

Conclusion and Implications

As the chapters in this book show, Singapore is a rare country where asset building is a major policy goal. Three examples include high

---

[41] Hillary Hui-Wen Hoo, *A study of the experience of debt, and of help received from FSCs for debt-related issues*, Honours Thesis, National University of Singapore, 2016.
[42] Abhijit V. Banerjee and Esther Duflo, *Poor economics: A radical rethinking of the way to fight global poverty* (New York: Perseus Books, 2011).

subsidies for public housing, CPF and Baby Bonus. The availability of these policies enables normative low-income households to build savings and own homes. Normative households refer to married couples with children and with CPF-contributing regular employment. Singles or single parents, and low-wage workers with informal and irregular jobs that do not pay CPF, have greater difficulty accessing these asset-building schemes.

Even if low-income families have access to assets, the assets are at very basic levels. For many, it takes extraordinary determination, self-control and discipline to sustain the savings or house. The margin for error is extremely small, and the wave of an external circumstance, e.g., a health episode or an unemployment spell or divorce, could propel them into a debt-ridden life leading eventually to the loss of the home or savings. Thus, the assets might instead be a burden, and well-being might instead be worsened by asset ownership. Further, these assets are only buffer stock for low-income families, rather than assets whose values appreciate. The regressivity of these asset-building policies drives wealth inequality instead of closing the gap.

At the root of the challenges that disable low-income families from owning and sustaining assets are low wages, disruptive labour markets and a high cost of living in Singapore. These have to be dealt with for asset building to reap its benefits with low-income families. The gig economy, for one, disrupts the labour market and the efforts to uplift wages and conditions of low-waged work. By contracting rather than employing workers, gig 'employers' do not need to contribute towards CPF or health insurance, or ensure wage bonuses or increments, thus shifting risks and asset building from employer to worker. This chapter has also argued that at the end of the day, universal policies are key to uplifting the poor. Asset-building policies can only help to inject some individual responsibility and defray some of the government's fiscal burden.

Strategies to help individuals keep building their assets can complement the necessary economic market and universal policies. Some strategies suggested by behavioural economics and poverty studies can be considered. First, information and communication of the information on asset-building programmes can be improved.

To low-income families, CPF and CDA might not be normative or salient. Regular information to low-income families using modes of communication familiar to them can improve the saliency and normalisation of the programmes. Second, commitment strategies can be drawn up with them, and accountability to the commitment plans can be set up via case management or self-help groups. One-off financial management workshops have limited effectiveness when the mental stress of living in poverty and debt depletes one's cognitive bandwidth. Friendly reminders instead become more effective. Third, case workers and social workers are instrumental to the first two strategies: to motivate the asset accumulation, encourage perseverance in building the asset, and find solutions and resources should exigencies arise.

In their roles as facilitator and encourager, the stance of case workers is important. Madsen (2007, p. 22) explains that with multi-stressed families, workers should actively cultivate "respect, connection, curiosity, and hope." This involves the worker recognising one's negative emotional reactions to clients. However, it also does not preclude confronting and taking a stand on important issues.

The accounts of the women interviewed by Hoo[43] stand in contrast to the stance described by Madsen. In Hoo's study, three respondents were so offended by condescending financial assistance staff that even though they had debts which the financial assistance could help, they refused to return for financial assistance. Instead, all eight respondents praised workers in Family Service Centres (FSCs), who helped clients cope with the mental stress of being in debt, but could offer little monetary assistance except to offer a voucher here or a free outing there. It must be noted that Hoo's study is of a small qualitative sample, and does not represent all financial assistance or FSC staff. However, the cases show the counter-productiveness of harsh workers who do not display understanding of the lived realities of poverty.

---

[43] Hillary Hui-Wen Hoo, *A study of the experience of debt, and of help received from FSCs for debt-related issues*, Honours Thesis. Singapore: National University of Singapore, 2016.

Putting together the contrast between Madsen and Hoo with the insights on cognitive bandwith by Mani, Mullainathan, Shafir and Zhao,[44] easing the way for clients becomes an important aim in case work and counselling. As opposed to the presupposition in public administration that provision of social assistance should be made difficult and unpleasant so that beneficiaries will not become welfare dependent, Behavioral Science suggests that we should ease the way to assistance in order to reduce the stress and cognitive load. Sherraden and colleagues further suggest that this improves hope and aspiration.

In conclusion, asset-building policies continue to hold much promise in helping low-income families improve economically. In Singapore, the very presence of asset-building policies provides a strong infrastructure. The design of the policies could be tweaked to factor in challenges that prevent asset building by low-income families. At the same time, asset building alone does not solve poverty. It might even become burdensome when families instead go into debt to build the assets. Essential are economic fundamentals of addressing market inequities and universal provision of basic levels of social protection. These policies have been initiated in recent years. They will need to gain momentum on one hand, but be balanced with competing policy priorities on the other hand.

Acknowledgements: I thank Joyce Lim for research assistance, and Tan Jian Qi and Grace Tan for help with the data. I thank Ng Kok Hoe for reviewing the paper. I thank my collaborators of the research studies cited in this article: Mathew Mathews, Ho Kong Weng, Ong Qiyan and Walter Theseira. I thank the Ministry of Social and Family Development for data reporting permission and factual checks. Any errors or opinions are however my own.

---

[44] Anandi Mani, Sendhil Mullainathan, Eldar Shafir and Jiaying Zhao, "Poverty impedes cognitive function".

Chapter 7

Water Policies as Assets

Yishu Zhou and Ching Leong

Introduction

Asset building is the creation of "conditions, as well as outlooks and behaviors, which together promote investments for household stability and social development" (Sherraden, 1991). While asset building most commonly refers to tangible conditions or infrastructure such as housing, education, or retirement security, this essay will argue that Singapore's state efforts to improve its water security also constitutes an essential part of its national asset-building policy.

In Michael Sherraden's view, asset building builds citizenship and nationhood by allowing individuals feel that they have a role to play in the well-being and development of the nation, resulting in a more participatory brand of citizenship. In the same vein, Alison Mathie and Gord Cunningham's[1] view of 'asset based community development' sees asset building as allowing individuals to own a stake in the development process, thus strengthening the social capital necessary to sustain citizenship. This is an increasingly important part of the state's legitimation process as globalisation and the increasingly free

---

[1] Alison Mathie and Gord Cunningham, "From clients to citizens: Asset-based community development as a strategy for community-driven development", *Development in Practice*, *13*(5), pp. 474–486, 2003.

movement of labour and capital has resulted in the gradual weakening of the social contract that governs people and nations.

Singapore's asset-building policies can be considered among the most advanced in the world. This is in part related to the circumstances of its founding. Since its independence in 1965, the Singapore national narrative had always revolved around the concept of vulnerability. In the earliest years of nation building, Singapore's split from Malaysia had rendered it with "no hinterland, no natural resources, and almost total dependence on Malaysia for water supplies."[2]

In many ways, the human right to water seems intuitive. Access to clean water is necessary for human well-being and survival. In many countries surrounded by freshwater resources, the question of water security may be far removed from the minds of most people. Water is also an infinitely renewable resource, which means that it recharges itself naturally during the water cycle.

In 1977, at the United Nations Water Conference held at Mar del Plata, Argentina, water was declared for first time as a human right. The resolution passed by the UN instructed that "All people whatever their stage of development and their social and economic conditions have the right to access to drinking water of quantities and of a quality equal to their basic needs."[3]

However, in Singapore, the presumption of water as a human right has never been expressed. Instead, water has always occupied a deeply personal and tumultuous space within Singapore's national consciousness.

In 1961 and 1962, Singapore signed two separate water agreements with Malaysia that would allow it to draw water from the Johor River, and which would expire in 2011 and 2061, respectively. Since then, talks held in attempt to establish new agreements have stalled, with Malaysian leaders periodically threatening to cut off Singapore's

---

[2] Cecilia Tortajada, Yugal Joshi and Asit K. Biswas, *The Singapore water story: Sustainable development in an urban city state* (London, England: Routledge, 2013).
[3] Asit K. Biswas, *Water development and management: Proceedings of the United Nations Water Conference, Mar Del Plata, Argentina, March 1977* (New York: Pergamon, 1978).

water supply (Long, 2001). This reflects what Yue Choong Kog, Ivan Fang Jau Lim and Joey Shi Ruey Long[4] refer to as 'hydropolitik', or the political exploitation of a 'life-and-death gambit' of a resource which is frequently described as a matter of national security.[5]

In this way, Singapore's relationship with its water as well as its narrative of water security bucks the larger trend of considering water as a human right. Rather, in moving away from rights-based discourse and into the domain of asset-building, Singapore policymakers have found a way to price water justly in ensuring access not only for the current generation but also for the ones to come.

Water Reimagined: Asset vs. Right

Singapore is known to be one of the world's driest countries, and was ranked by the World Resources Institute as the fifth most water-stressed country in the world, narrowly behind other arid nations such as Bahrain, Kuwait, and Qatar.[6] As it has no natural water resources to speak of, water is imported from Malaysia, as stipulated by a contract that is due to expire in 2061. Water is often a source of political tension between the two countries, and attempts to renew the water contract beyond 2061 have been strained and intermittent.

Yet, Singapore's overall water policies have been, on many fronts, successful. All residents have 24-hour access to clean and safe supply of water piped to their homes, and water quality is strictly regulated by the national water utility, the Public Utilities Board (PUB), according to World Health Organization standards. Non-revenue water is impressively low,

---

[4] Yue Choong Kog, Ivan Fang Jau Lim and Joey Shi Ruey Long, "Beyond vulnerability? Water in Singapore–Malaysia relations, *Institute of Defence and Strategic Studies Monograph, No. 3* (Singapore: Institute of Defence and Strategic Studies, 2002).

[5] M. Falkenmark, "Fresh water: Time for a modified approach", *Ambio*, pp. 192–200, 1986; Peter H. Gleick, *Water in crisis: A guide to the world's fresh water resources* (Oxford, England: Oxford University Press, 1993).

[6] Andrew Maddocks, Robert Samuel Young and Paul Reig, *Ranking the world's most water-stressed countries in 2040*, World Resources Institute, 26 August 2015.

accounting for just 5% in 2015[7], one of the lowest even among other developed countries.

Many international agencies have also noted the island's strong performance in comparative studies. One especially illuminating indicator is the Asian Development Bank's IDWA (Index of Drinking Water Adequacy).[8] Under the IDWA, Singapore scores full marks (100) in four out of five indices — in access, capacity, use, and quality. None of the 23 countries captured on the index have such impressive scores. Indeed, if not for its poor resource endowment (a score of only 42), Singapore would have topped the table of member countries.

A common refrain in rights-based discourse stipulates that the right to water contains both entitlements and freedoms. Entitlements refer to access to the minimum amount of safe drinking water required for survival and health; while freedoms include protection from disruption or interference with the water supply.[9] However, this definition fails to make the distinction between water as a right and water as a resource that has to be managed, governed, and allocated in a just and equitable manner. The cost of water has much less to do with 'raw' water, or 'water in nature',[10] and more with the management of water in ensuring that such entitlements and freedoms can be carried out.

Further, discussions of water governance often present a false dichotomy between water as a right and water as a commodity. The declaration of water as a human right is neither necessary nor sufficient in ensuring the adequate provision of water; nor does pricing water lend itself to the slippery slope of the neo-liberalisation of environmental resources. Rather, Garrett Hardin's essay on the 'tragedy

---

[7] Public Utilities Board, *Our Water, The Flow of Progress: Annual Report 2014/2015* (Singapore: The Author, 2014/2015).
[8] Seetharam Kallidaikurichi and Bhanoji Rao, "Index of drinking water adequacy for the Asian economies", *Water Policy*, *12*(S1), pp. 135–154, 2010.
[9] Nandita Singh, "Introduction", in Nandita Singh (ed.), *The human right to water: From concept to reality* (New York: Springer, 2016).
[10] Brent M. Haddad, *Rivers of gold: Designing markets to allocate water in California* (Covelo, CA: Island Press, 1999).

of the commons'[11] is instructive in illustrating the dilemma that arises in the distribution of public goods. Especially in the case of environmental resources, which carry an intangible cost, limits must be delineated in order to ensure equity and sustainability.

In this case, what can be done is to make the crucial distinction between 'open access' to 'common property'.[12] While 'open access' implies that anyone can stake their claim to the resource, 'common property' implies that access is guarded by an owner, such as the state. This brings our thinking closer to conceiving of water as an asset. The PUB is in a fortunate position of dealing with a populace who are used to paying for water because the island buys the majority of its water supply from Malaysia. The notion of property rights prepares the consumer to ascribe a value to water.

Therefore, in Singapore, everyone who uses water is charged from the first drop. While the water is not free, the government has targeted subsidies under a scheme called RUAS (Rent and Utilities Assistance Scheme) where the poor receive subsidies for their utilities. Even for the very poor, the water connection is 24/7, and at the service level the same as that experienced by all other Singaporeans. The water bill is priced progressively, depending on the amount of water used per household.

Water is also affordable, constituting just 1% of the average household expenditure in median income households and 2% of the average household expenditure for households with income in the bottom quintile,[13] before the application of rebates and subsidies. In 2017, water tariffs in Singapore were increased by 30% for the first time in 20 years, to accommodate for the higher costs of water production and PUB's larger investments in new water technologies and infrastructure projects. However, the PUB has assured lower-income households that

---

[11] Garrett Hardin, "The tragedy of the commons", *Journal of Natural Resources Policy Research*, 1(3), pp. 243–253, 2009.

[12] David Pearce, *Blueprint 4: Capturing global environmental value* (London, England: Earthscan, 1995).

[13] Department of Statistics, Ministry of Trade and Industry, *Report on the household expenditure survey 2012/2013* (Singapore: The Author, 2014).

they will see no change in their water bill, and rebates will be made available to offset the higher costs of water.

The conception of water as an asset thus also informs how Singapore approaches the issue of pricing. There are many ways to price water. The most straightforward way is to recover the cost of production, including the cost of treating wastewater, in line with what institutions such as the Asian Development Bank advocate. Another is to include the cost to the environment, encapsulated as 'environmental capital',[14] a common good which nonetheless can be priced. Singapore has chosen a third route — to monetise a strategic variable.

As such, its tariffs reflect not just the cost of water supply but also the cost of the next alternative source of water: desalination. This is billed as the water conservation tax, which constitutes about 35% of the total water bill. This is emblematic of the asset-building approach, for it embeds a social investment function into the pricing of water, allowing citizens to feel that they have an ownership and responsibility not only for the water resources but also the assuredness of their continued security and sustainability.

Water in short is priced as an *economic* virtue. At the same time, it should be free to those who cannot pay because of a *moral* imperative that is sometimes encapsulated by the declaration that it is a human right. The 'water as asset' designation encapsulates both the economic logic of charging for water, and the understanding that it is a public good necessary for human life and health. However, it also introduces another crucial dimension. By reframing water as an asset, the price of water is understood to encapsulate not only the cost of water now, but the capital necessary to construe water as an investment that would yield future benefits.

This not only allows policy makers to take a long-term approach in pricing water resources, but also strengthens the social contract and ensures inclusivity in making all citizens feel that they are contributing to, and benefiting from, the country's development.

---

[14] Peter M. Clarkson, Yue Li and Gordon D. Richardson, "The market valuation of environmental capital expenditures by pulp and paper companies", *The Accounting Review*, 79(2), pp. 329–353, 2004.

Water as Asset Building in Singapore

A crucial factor differentiates water from other asset-building instruments. While the broadest definition of an 'asset' refers to "stored-up purchasing power ... it reflects savings and investments that can be drawn on in times of need"[15], assets within the paradigm of nation building often refer more specifically to material or tangible assets, often those which translate into financial or social security, such as housing, education, childcare plans, or retirement benefits. These elements are relevant and relatable, and have a perceptible role to play in affecting quality of life.

Water, on the other hand, is a shared resource, and one which feels both immediate and abstract. Working backwards from Sherraden's definition that assets are resources that contribute to long-term social and economic development,[16] it is apparent that water — and environmental resources in general — ought to qualify. The challenge therefore is to prompt consumers to attribute a value to water: not just a generalist perspective on the overall benefits of water, but a personal stake and investment in water as a valuable resource, as much as a savings account or mortgage on a house.

This would involve a valuation of environmental stewardship, or in other words, how much people are willing to pay to conserve and invest in the continued provision of clean water. Behavioural economics makes the crucial distinction between what one is willing to pay for X and what one is willing to accept for it. The latter is generally higher than the former. One hypothesis formulated to account for this behaviour is the 'endowment effect' — that when one is endowed with something, possession creates additional value which is not present when X is on the shelf. The endowment effect can be applied to consumer behaviour by finding a way for consumers to feel that they *possess* the environment in some general way. In this

---

[15] Melvin L. Oliver and Thomas M. Shapiro, "Wealth of a nation", *American Journal of Economics and Sociology*, *49*(2), p. 131, 1990.
[16] Michael Sherraden, Li Zou, Ben Hok-bun Ku, Suo Deng and Sibin Wang (eds.), *Asset-building policies and innovations in Asia (Vol. 3)* (London, England: Routledge, 2014).

way, what they are willing to accept for a unit of depletion (or loss) of environmental capital would be more than what they are willing to pay for it (gain).

The endowment effect results from one's possession of a good. Although we paid $Y for a certain good X, we are less willing to part with X for the same amount, purely on the basis that we now own X. According to Jack L. Knetsch and J.A. Sinden, the endowment effect is explained in this way: "The observed reluctance to give up money or assets seems likely to be, at least in part, due to various cognitive biases and such motives as an incentive to provide against a feeling of regret that might accompany a deliberately made change in asset position."[17] A second force operating in the endowment effect is the 'sense of entitlement' that we have acquired a right to X by virtue of ownership which needs to be compensated for.

How then can we 'take possession' of the environment in a meaningful way? Suzanne G. Thompson and Michelle A. Barton's[18] conception of the ecocentric–anthropocentric scale identifies two main ways people conceive of and attribute value to their environment. Ecocentric individuals find inherent value in nature, and believe that nature is worthy of preservation as an end in itself. Anthropocentric individuals view nature primarily as the source of natural resources, and the means from which the ends of human comfort and quality of life may be extracted and maintained. These values translate into perceptions and beliefs, which form the basis for subsequent actions. This understanding of how people relate to their environment thus lends traction to the 'value-belief-norm' theory,[19] which posits a causal chain that links the actions of individuals to their personal beliefs.

---

[17] Jack L. Knetsch and J.A. Sinden, "Willingness to pay and compensation demanded: Experimental evidence of an unexpected disparity in measures of value", *The Quarterly Journal of Economics*, *99*(3), p. 517, 1984.

[18] Suzanne G. Thompson and Michelle A. Barton, "Ecocentric and anthropocentric attitudes toward the environment", *Journal of Environmental Psychology*, *14*(2), pp. 149–157, 1994.

[19] Paul C. Stern, Thomas Dietz, Troy Abel, Gregory A. Guagnano and Linda Kalof, "A value-belief-norm theory of support for social movements: The case of environmentalism", *Human Ecology Review*, *6*(2), pp. 81–97, 1999.

In Singapore, there are several literal ways in which this notion of 'taking possession' of the environment has been seen in public policy. For example, school children often adopt national parks around their school — they take responsibility for their landscaping and future development, as well as lead guided tours through the park. The policy maker's intention, when this scheme was launched in 1997, was to create a community outreach programme "aimed at inculcating a sense of ownership and responsibility for parks among participants." Another way it has done so is to ask people to plant trees — anyone who pays the National Parks Board gets to plant a tree, and the board will look after the tree for life. Now the Board of course can plant trees itself, and the S$200 does not defray much of the cost of caring for the tree for any length of time. But this public effort has the effect of allowing people to feel that they own a tree.

Relating this to water, Singapore has four main sources of water supply — what is commonly known as the 'Four National Taps', as introduced in 2005. Under this strategy, Singapore expanded its water resources from imported water and water from local catchments to include desalination and recycled wastewater (also known as NEWater). There are currently two desalination plants in operation, which are able to meet up to 25% of Singapore's water demands. By 2020, there will be five desalination plants built, meeting up to 30% of Singapore's water needs. Singapore also has five NEWater plants which combined can fulfil up to 40% of Singapore's water demand, with an aim of increasing this to 55% in the long run. It is envisioned that under this strategy, Singapore's reliance on imported water will be gradually reduced until 2061, when Singapore's water agreement with Johor would have expired, and the country would then become self-sufficient, thus effectively 'closing the water-loop'.[20]

The diversification of its water resources is a perennial source of national pride for Singaporeans. Because of the deeply political nature

---

[20] Teng Chye Khoo, "Singapore water: Yesterday, today and tomorrow", in Asit K. Biswas, Cecilia Tortajada and Rafael Izquierdo (eds.), *Water management in 2020 and beyond* (pp. 237–250) (Berlin Heidelberg: Springer, 2009).

of water in Singapore, and the 'life and death challenges'[21] that come with the problem to sustain sustainable water resources, the prospect of achieving water independence is a much more profound one. NEWater shines particularly bright as a technology and policy innovation, because it has the greatest potential to 'close the water loop' and ensure water self-sufficiency, and is also cheaper and more energy efficient than desalination. More importantly, the successful integration of recycled water into the water supply makes Singapore's case a rarity and distinction, which was in no small part abetted by the fact that policymakers reminded the local population that recycled water has to be one of their sources.[22]

Looking into the future, the strategic thrust of Singapore's water policy is encompassed in its ABC (Active, Beautiful, Clean) Waters to build an intimate sense of ownership among its people for keeping water catchments clean. This sense of ownership is an essential part of the success of water policies, because with its small size, two-thirds of the island will eventually be turned into water catchment areas. As then Minister for the Environment and Water Resources Dr. Yaacob Ibrahim put it, "When people value our water more, they would want to conserve it and keep it clean."[23] If indeed the WTA is much higher than the WTP, then Singapore would have succeeded in building shared norms and values towards environmental behavior, in internalizing shared water resources as an asset.

Conclusion

In this essay, we have identified water to be a key asset — both material and immaterial — in the stability of Singapore's development as well

---

[21] Yu-Min Joo and Yee-Kuang Heng, "Turning on the taps: Singapore's new branding as a global hydrohub", *International Development Planning Review*, 39(2), pp. 209–227, 2017.
[22] Cecilia Tortajada, Yugal Joshi and Asit K. Biswas, *The Singapore water story: Sustainable development in an urban city state.*
[23] See Speech by Dr. Yacoob Ibrahim, Minister for the Environment and Water Resources, at the Committee of Supply Debate 2005, Part 1, 8 March 2005.

as its continuous nation building enterprise. We theorise on the deeply symbolic and political nature of water in Singapore's national consciousness, as well as how it has been closely linked to nation building since independence, and further aggrandised by the faltering water negotiation talks with Malaysia. We thus argue that dominant water rights discourse is not strictly applicable in the Singapore case. We then introduce the concept of asset building, and apply it to Singapore's water policies in showing firstly, that Singapore has utilised the asset-building approach to enhance its water security; and further, that 'assets' need not necessarily refer to ownership in the material sense of the word. By utilising examples from Singapore's development experience, we show how water can be used as a point of social cohesion in strengthening a collectivist and participatory type of citizenship.

Chapter 8

Conscription and Its Contribution to Singapore

Bernard F.W. Loo

Introduction

The policy of conscription, otherwise called National Service (NS), has provided the foundation stone for the defence of Singapore. Conscription has undergone a remarkable transformation, from a policy that was widely disliked by the population to one that is today widely embraced as important and valuable in ways that transcend the mere imperative of defending a sovereign state.[1] However, it is often forgotten that conscription was not the policy option that Singapore's first Minister for Defence Dr. Goh Keng Swee had recommended. Rather, based on the advice of the Israeli military advisors that had helped to build up the Singapore Armed Forces (SAF), he had

---

[1] According to a survey conducted by the Institute of Policy Studies, 98% of respondents indicated that National Service (NS) is essential for the defence and security of Singapore, which itself is essential for the economic success of the state. In the survey, 95% of respondents also saw positive personal growth outcomes for Singaporean males, NS being the voyage that takes Singaporean males from boyhood to manhood. See Chan-Hoong Leong, Wai Wai Yang and Henry Mun Wah Ho, *Singaporean attitudes to National Service* (Singapore: Institute of Policy Studies, Lee Kuan Yew School of Public Policy, National University of Singapore, 2014).

proposed an all-volunteer army comprising 12 battalions to be raised between 1966 and 1969. It was the first Prime Minister, Mr. Lee Kuan Yew, who had insisted on conscription as the basis for the raising of the SAF.[2] Nevertheless, it is Dr. Goh who goes down in history as the architect who built the SAF.[3]

However, attitudes towards the principle of military conscription have waxed and waned, especially since the end of the Cold War. Ideas about the peace dividend deriving in post-Cold War period, the interstate peace that stems from either the proliferation of democratic governance or economic interdependence have made the notion that states have to defend their existence against existing or potential threats seem outdated.[4] A number of countries that previously maintained military conscription had also either suspended or abolished this policy. Given this backdrop, it is fair to ask what has NS done for Singapore.

This study lays out a three-point argument that connects the security perceptions of Singapore's policy makers and the policy of NS. It will begin by outlining how Singaporean policy makers, Dr. Goh in particular, perceived the strategic environment to be like. Next the study will outline how the SAF has developed throughout its existence into a military that is today widely held as the most modern and most well-equipped military organisation in Southeast Asia. Next, this study will briefly examine the extent to which the commitment to NS and the maintenance of a fairly sizeable SAF has impacted on the other fundamental national interest of growing the economy. Finally,

---

[2] Kuan Yew Lee, *From Third World to First: The Singapore Story 1965–2000* (Singapore: Marshall Cavendish and The Straits Times Press, 2000), p. 35.

[3] See Bernard Fook Weng Loo, "Goh Keng Swee and the emergence of a modern SAF: The rearing of a poisonous shrimp", in Emrys Chew and Chong Guan Kwa (eds.), *Goh Keng Swee: A legacy of public service* (pp. 127–152) (Singapore: World Scientific, 2012).

[4] For democratic peace theory, see, for instance Azar Gat, "The democratic peace theory reframed: The impact of modernity", *World Politics*, 58(1), pp. 73–100, October 2005. For interdependent peace theory, see for instance Andrew Moravcsik, "Taking preferences seriously: A liberal theory of international politics", *International Organization*, 51(4), pp. 513–533, Autumn 1997.

this study will examine the relationship between NS and the greater national project of nation building.

Perceiving the Security Environment

While the aforementioned question may appear facetious, it is nevertheless important to establish the mindset of the first-generation policy makers in their decision to implement conscription in favour of the Israeli proposal of an all-volunteer SAF. This mindset was encapsulated in a speech in Parliament on 23 December 1965 by then Defence Minister Dr. Goh, in which he stated, "It is no use pretending that without the British military presence in Singapore today, the island cannot be easily overrun by any neighbouring country within a radius of a thousand miles." Up to 1970, British troops were stationed in Singapore to safeguard the island's external defence, but the SAF had only two infantry battalions "for [her] protection in normal times."[5] The SAF, clearly, was not in a position to by itself do very much in terms of defending the island against external aggression.

Given the strategic circumstances that surrounded Singapore's emergence as a sovereign state, this mindset was understandable. The ideological conflict that was the Cold War manifested itself in Southeast Asia in a hot war that was the Vietnam War. This ideological conflict was further manifested locally in the continued existence of the Malayan Communist Party (MCP), which although having been roundly defeated in the first Malayan Emergency, had not disavowed its ultimate goal of establishing a communist state in Malaysia and Singapore.[6]

---

[5] "Military spending modest and purely for defence", *The Straits Times*, 6 December 1967, p. 8.

[6] Teik Soon Lau, "National threat perceptions of Singapore", in Charles Morrison (ed.), *Threats to security in East Asia-Pacific: National and regional perspectives* (Lexington, MA: Lexington Books, 1983), p. 116; Bilveer Singh, "Singapore's management of its security problems", *Asia-Pacific Community*, 29, Summer 1985, p. 81; and Yuan-li Wu, "Planning security for a small nation: Lessons from Singapore", *Pacific Community*, 3(4), 1972, p. 663.

Away from the ideological conflict, there was the history of *Konfrontasi* with Indonesia[7] and threats from Malaysia, the latter in particular looming large in Singapore's security calculus. The acrimonious separation and the subsequent strained relations across the Causeway meant that Mr. Lee and Dr. Goh could not rule out the possibility of a threat to Singapore arising out of Malaysia.[8] Malaysian politicians had felt that Kuala Lumpur (KL) had a natural right to ensure that Singapore would not undertake any policies prejudicial to Malaysian interests. There were concerns about the possibility of the Malaysian Army invading Singapore to "take Singapore back into the Federation forcibly."[9] Alternatively, "Malay ultras [could] instigate a coup … and reverse the independence we had acquired."[10] There were apparent threats from Malaysia to use Singapore's dependence on Malaysia for its potable water — what Mr. Lee referred to as "rash political acts"[11] and "random act of madness"[12] — as a lever against Singapore adopting policies that would be "prejudicial to Malaysia's interests."[13] It is difficult to not conclude that the dominant image was one of potential trouble that could directly or indirectly affect the security of Singapore.[14]

---

[7] Felix Chang, "In defense of Singapore", *Orbis*, Winter 2003, p. 108; Teik Soon Lau, "National threat perceptions of Singapore", p. 122; and Kuan Yew Lee, *From Third World to First: The Singapore Story 1965–2000*, p. 20; Michael Leifer, *Singapore's foreign policy: Coping with vulnerability* (New York: Routledge, 2000), p. 2.

[8] Chin Kin Wah, "Reflections on the shaping of strategic cultures in Southeast Asia", in Derek da Cunha (ed.), *Southeast Asian perspectives on security* (Singapore: Institute of Southeast Asian Studies, 2000), p. 7; and Bilveer Singh, "Singapore's management of its security problems", p. 85.

[9] Kuan Yew Lee, *From Third World to First: The Singapore Story 1965–2000*, p. 24; Michael Leifer, *Singapore's foreign policy: Coping with vulnerability*, p. 53.

[10] Kuan Yew Lee, *From Third World to First: The Singapore Story 1965–2000*, p. 22.

[11] Kuan Yew Lee, *From Third World to First: The Singapore Story 1965–2000*, p. 46.

[12] Kuan Yew Lee, *From Third World to First: The Singapore Story 1965–2000*, p. 276.

[13] Chong Guan Kwa, "Introduction", in Chong Guan Kwa (ed.), *Beyond vulnerability? Water in Singapore — Malaysia relations* (Singapore: Institute of Defence and Strategic Studies, 2002), p. 4; see also Michael Leifer, *Singapore's foreign policy: Coping with vulnerability*, p. 19.

[14] See Kuan Yew Lee, *From Third World to First: The Singapore Story 1965–2000*, p. 24; Michael Leifer, *Singapore's foreign policy: Coping with vulnerability*, p. 53.

The geography of Singapore lies at the heart of this sense of vulnerability. In contrast to its immediate neighbours, Singapore lacks geostrategic depth, stemming from its small geophysical size. Singapore's territorial waters are almost completely surrounded by the territorial waters of Indonesia and Malaysia.[15] Singapore's geopolitical position, sitting astride the trade routes connecting the Pacific and Indian oceans, also makes the island a potentially attractive target for any other state seeking to control the maritime trade that traverses these oceans.[16] If nothing else, the geostrategic position of Singapore meant that any instability arising out of its weaknesses would strengthen the temptation of external actors to intervene. As Dr. Goh said in a speech in Parliament on 13 March 1967, "If you are in a completely vulnerable position anyone disposed to do so can hold you to ransom, and life for you will become very tiresome .... Small states are likely to be a great source of trouble in the world if they cannot look after themselves. If the management of their domestic affairs is

---

See also Derek da Cunha (ed.), *Southeast Asian perspectives on security* (Singapore: Institute of Southeast Asian Studies, 2000); Alom Peled, *Soldiers apart: A study of ethnic military manpower policies in Singapore, Israel and South Africa* (Ann Arbor, MI: University Microfilms International, 1994), pp. 60–65; and Bilveer Singh, *The vulnerability of small states revisited: A study of Singapore's post-Cold War foreign policy* (Yogyakarta, Indonesia: Gajah Mada University Press, 1999). Since many Malaysian leaders opposed Singapore's independence, Malaysia took various steps to exploit Singapore's lack of military preparation between 1965 and 1969, which reinforced Singapore's sense of vulnerability by playing on the possibility of a Malaysian invasion. Malaysian politicians tried to prevent Singapore from building a strong military that could threaten Malaysia, such that Singapore had to quietly develop a military force. Furthermore, Malaysia had refused to evacuate its troops in Singapore and release Singaporeans then serving in the Malaysian Armed Forces, until heavy British pressure and intense political bargaining between the three governments resolved these issues.

[15] Tim Huxley, *Defending the Lion City: The Armed Forces of Singapore* (St Leonards, NSW: Allen and Unwin, 2000).

[16] See Richard Deck, "Singapore: Comprehensive Security — Total Defence", in Ken Booth and Russel D. Troud (eds.), Strategic cultures in the Asia-Pacific region (New York: St. Martin's Press, 1999), pp. 248–249; Tim Huxley, *Defending the Lion City: The Armed Forces of Singapore*, pp. 31–33.

so bad as to invite civil war and disorder, there is always the risk that larger states may be tempted to intervene." The domestic security environment was similarly bleak. Apart from the continuing threat posed by the MCP, communal politics was problematic.[17] There had already been two major incidents of communal violence in Singapore, the Maria Hertogh riots and the 1964 riots.[18] While these threats were largely domestic, they were nevertheless part of a symbiotic relationship with the external strategic environment. A constant image that has run through Singapore's strategic culture of vulnerability is that of a "Chinese island in a Malay sea".[19] Being located within an essentially Malay and Muslim archipelago, Singapore was extremely mindful that 'Chinese chauvinism' could adversely affect its relations with Malaysia and Indonesia and give both countries an excuse to intervene on behalf of the Malay-Muslim population in Singapore.[20] Similarly, 'Malay chauvinism' represented a potential threat to Singapore in the form of Islamist fundamentalist movements.[21]

Delivering on Defence and Security?

Given these uncertainties in the internal and external strategic environment, Singapore needed to develop an SAF that can defend Singapore; this was clearly no easy task. At the point of independence, the SAF was a very small force of two infantry battalions with no significant armoured or artillery forces, let alone credible air or naval capabilities. As a first step, manpower resources had to be increased. The solution was conscription.[22] This was absolutely critical for the task of developing an indigenous capacity to defend the nascent state.

---

[17] Heng Chee Chan and Obaid Ul Haq (eds.), *The prophetic and the political: Selected speeches and writings of S. Rajaratnam* (New York: St. Martin's Press, 1987), p. 105.

[18] Jürgen Haacke, *ASEAN's diplomatic and security culture: Origins, development and prospects* (New York: RoutledgeCurzon, 2003), p. 39.

[19] Kuan Yew Lee, *From Third World to First: The Singapore Story 1965–2000*, p. 15; see also Derek da Cunha (ed.), *Southeast Asian perspectives on security*, p. 134.

[20] Bilveer Singh, "Singapore's management of its security problems", pp. 83–84.

[21] Teik Soon Lau, "National threat perceptions of Singapore", p. 120.

[22] Heng Chee Chan, *Singapore: The politics of survival 1965–1967* (Singapore: Oxford University Press, 1971), p. 48.

Table 8.1. Defence expenditure by years, 1970–2010

	1970	1980	1990	2000	2010
Expenditure	1,053	1,949	4,246	7,860	85,494
% of GDP	4.3	4.7	3.8	4.4	3.1

Note: Expenditure expressed in constant USD millions.
Source: Stockholm International Peace Research Institute (2017).

Conscription was underpinned by an on-going commitment to support a relatively high level of military spending to acquire the necessary military hardware (see Table 8.1). This commitment to support a relatively high defence expenditure signalled Singapore's resolve to address its vulnerabilities.

This high level of defence spending allowed the SAF to transition from its first-generation incarnation — the so-called 'poisonous shrimp', where the SAF sought to defend the island at the water's edge first, to be followed by a 'Stalingrad-style of close combat' in urban areas, aiming to make the human and material costs of aggression against Singapore to unacceptable levels[23] — to its current third-generation incarnation (see Table 8.2). The SAF today fields the most modern armed forces. However, its navy's submarine fleet is ageing. Nevertheless, there are already plans for this submarine fleet to be replaced with Type-218SG submarines.[24] Singapore has a fleet of 32 F-15SGs, and its F-16C/Ds have undergone periodic upgrading.[25] Its F-5 fleet will need to be replaced, and there has been speculation that Singapore will eventually acquire a number of F-35 combat aircraft.[26] Its land forces currently field

---

[23] Deck, "Singapore: Comprehensive Security — Total Defence", p. 249.

[24] Kelvin Wong, "TKMS starts construction of Singapore's Type 218SG submarines", *IHS Jane's 360*, 28 June 2015 Retrieved on 21 March 2016 from http://www.janes.com/article/52609/tkms-starts-construction-of-singapore-s-type-218sg-submarines.

[25] Mike Yeo, "RSAF forms 2nd local F-15SG squadron", *IHS Jane's 360*, 22 March 2016. Retrieved on 23 March 2016 from http://www.janes.com/article/58959/rsaf-forms-second-local-f-15sg-squadron

[26] Kok Fai Loke, "F-35 fighter jet to go on display at Singapore Airshow", *Channel NewsAsia*, 9 February 2016. Retrieved on 21 March 2016 from http://www.channelnewsasia.com/news/singapore/f-35-fighter-jet-to-go-on/2501102.html

Table 8.2.   Singapore's weapon system

Weapon system	Designation	No. acquired	Year acquired/delivered
Main battle tank	Leopard II	96	2007/2007–2012
Submarine	Challenger	3+1	1995–1997/1997–2001
	Archer	2	2005/2011–2012
Frigate	Formidable	6	2000/2007–2009
Combat aircraft	F-5E	29	1976–1980/1979–1985
	F-15SG	32	2005–2013/2009–2014
	F-16C/D	80	1994–2000/1998–2005

Sources: International Institute for Strategic Studies; Stockholm International Peace Research Institute.

recently-acquired Leopard II main battle tanks; and, while it is not reflected in Table 8.2, it also fields 155mm howitzers and infantry fighting vehicles/armed personnel carriers that are indigenously designed and built.[27]

That the SAF today is unrecognisable from its incarnation in 1965 can be explained by two factors. One, the process of building, maintaining and occasionally upgrading an armed forces is called the arms dynamic, precisely because it is a dynamic process.[28] An armed forces is not a sculpture, after all. Two, the 'Stalingrad-style of close combat' that the 'poisonous shrimp' strategy suggested was, ultimately, defeatist. Given Singapore's lack of geostrategic depth, the only military posture that makes strategic sense is one that emphasises offensive military operations as part of a pre-emptive deterrent strategy.[29]

---

[27] Singapore's indigenous defence industries may be an example of what Richard Bitzinger calls technonationalism; see Richard Bitzinger, "Defense industries in Asia and the technonationalist impulse", *Contemporary Security Policy*, 36(3), pp. 453–472, 2015.

[28] Barry Buzan and Eric Herring, *The arms dynamic in world politics* (Boulder, CO and London, England: Lynne Rienner, 1998).

[29] Tim Huxley, *Defending the Lion City: The Armed Forces of Singapore*, p. 56.

Guns and Butter, Not Guns versus Butter?[30]

Arguably, this security exists both as a public good in itself, but also exists to provide the basis of another public good, namely economic prosperity. Lee Kuan Yew said to at the Temasek Society's 30th Anniverary dinner in 2012, "Without a strong SAF, there is no economic future, there is no security." This correlation between national security and economic growth — and foreign direct investment (FDI) being seen as the critical driver of economic growth for Singapre — is a message that successive generations of policy makers have made. This 'guns and butter, not guns versus butter' approach is not without merit. Emile Benoit's studies of developing economies in 1950s and 1960s demonstrate that developing countries with the highest levels of defence expenditure also tended to have the highest economic growth rates, and that concomitantly, countries that spent the least on defence had the lowest economic growth rates.[31]

Granted, in relation to its immediate neighbours, Singapore's military expenditure imposed a greater burden on its economy; that being said, it is arguably also an economically sustainable burden (see Table 8.3). Singapore commits to a policy to support a relatively high level of military expenditure, certainly in comparison to its immediate neighbours, but the absolute size of its military expenditure is driven by the size of the Singapore economy. In its initial years, Singapore's military expenditure was, admittedly, a greater burden on its fledgling economy — in 1968, military expenditure amounted to six percent of its GDP,[32] but as Table 8.3 demonstrates, military expenditure has imposed a decreasing burden on the economy, without sacrificing the

---

[30] The discussion here is taken from Adrian Kuah and Bernard Loo, "Examining the defence industrialization — Economic growth relationship: The case of Singapore", IDSS Working Paper No. 70, July 2004.

[31] Emile Benoit, *Defense and economic growth in developing countries* (Lexington, KY: Lexington Books, 1973); and Emile Benoit, "Growth and defense in developing countries", *Economic Development and Cultural Change*, 26, pp. 271–280, 1978.

[32] Tim Huxley, *Defending the Lion City: The Armed Forces of Singapore*, p. 27.

Table 8.3. Defence expenditure as percentage of GDP: A comparison

Country	1970	1980	1990	2000	2010
Indonesia	—	2.9%	1.4%	0.7%	0.6%
Malaysia	5.2%	4.2%	2.6%	1.6%	1.5%
Singapore	5.4%	4.6%	4.6%	4.5%	3.4%

Source: Stockholm International Peace Research Institute.

absolute amount of money devoted to military spending.[33] This consideration of financial prudence in determining the country's military expenditure is a legacy that can be attributed to its first Defence Minister, Dr. Goh Keng Swee.

This prudence would not have been possible without NS providing the basis of the manpower that was considered by military planners and policy makers to be necessary for the defence and security of Singapore. To be able to build an all-volunteer professional armed forces would have required an even greater military expenditure than Singapore's policy makers have been prepared to accept. The global experience demonstrates that in countries that maintain all-volunteer professional armed forces, the majority of military expenditure goes towards salaries. This is intuitive, as military organisations need to offer salaries that are competitive with the civilian economy to attract sufficient numbers of men and women into military service. If Singapore's policy makers had accepted the Israeli military advisors' recommendations for an all-volunteer professional armed forces, it is reasonable to conclude that Singapore's military expenditures would have had to be even greater than they have been. NS, arguably, contributed to keep the defence budget within economically sustainable limits.

Finally, the Singapore experience demonstrates that the positive correlation between military expenditure and economic growth is not

---

[33] One study suggests that Singapore's defence spending between 1969 and 1978 had grown by 114%, even while the economic burden was kept relatively static. See Sukhumbhand Paribatra and Chai-Anan Samudavanija, "Internal dimensions of regional security in Southeast Asia", in Mohammed Ayoob (ed.), *Regional security in the Third World: Case studies from Southeast Asia and the Middle East* (London, England: Croom Helm, 1986), p. 79.

down solely to the ability to attract FDI. In principle, any military organisation can act as a competitor with the civilian economy for access to the pool of human resources available in the country.[34] There is some evidence that supports this claim. During periods of economic recession, the SAF was able to reduce overall unemployment, especially with the case of lower-educated Singaporeans.[35] Admittedly this number of people who might have otherwise been employed in the civilian economy is small.

Conscription and Nation-Building[36]

Finally, conscription provided the fledgling country a platform from which to help build a national consciousness and national identity. This benefit that conscription afforded was acknowledged as an equally important policy objective that underpinned the decision to adopt universal conscription. As Dr. Goh Keng Swee argued in Parliament on 13 March 1967, "Nothing creates loyalty and national consciousness more speedily and more thoroughly than participation in defence and membership of the armed forces." As Dr. Goh subsequently noted in a speech on 29 November 1969,

In Singapore, we are not yet a close-knit community; so many of our people are of recent migrant origin. All of this goes towards creating a sense of values which is personal, self-centred with anti-social tendencies

---

[34] See, for instance Yong Mun Cheong, "The military and development in Singapore", in J. Soedjati Djiwandono and Yong Mun Cheong (eds.), *Soldiers and stability in Southeast Asia* (Singapore: Institute of Southeast Asian Studies, 1988), p. 287.

[35] Between 1984 and 1985, SAF enlistments of other ranks up to Warrant Officer increased from 1,851 to 2,304; during that period, the number of personnel who opted to renew their military contract service increased from 539 to 711. See Kin Wah Chin, "Singapore: Threat perception and defence spending in a city-state", in Kin Wah Chin (ed.), *Defence spending in Southeast Asia* (Singapore: Institute of Southeast Asian Studies, 1987), p. 217.

[36] Much of the analysis in this section comes from a prior publication. See Bernard Fook Weng Loo, "Goh Keng Swee and the emergence of a modern SAF: The rearing of a poisonous shrimp", in Emrys Chew and Chong Guan Kwa (eds.), *Goh Keng Swee: A legacy of public service* (pp. 127–152) (Singapore: World Scientific, 2012).

where a conflict arises between personal interest and social obligations. There are the values of a rootless parvenu society. We cannot hope to remove them overnight, but in the process of creating a stronger national consciousness among our people, we will find that military service will play an increasingly important role, as it has played in other nations and in other ages.

It was part of a broader national objective of survival. National survival was simply a function of the military capacity to defend oneself; it was also a function of the extent to which the population at large felt connected to the island. This sense of connection was absolutely necessary, if the population was to be successfully mobilised to undertake not only the military tasks of nation building, but the other aspects discussed elsewhere in this volume. In a sense, therefore, Dr. Goh was conscious of not only the defence and security needs, but how answering these needs plugged into wider concerns within the overall project of nation-building.

NS was not a popular decision. Given the demographics of Singapore's population, with a large majority of its population being of Chinese ethnicity, there were initial cultural aversions to military service. The first-generation policy makers were aware of this condition, as evidenced by Dr. Goh in Parliament on 23 December 1965: "There is a common saying among the Chinese masses which goes ... 'Good men do not become soldiers, good iron does not make nails'." Furthermore, this resistance to military training was not culturally specific to the ethnic Chinese population.

Given these widely held cultural aversions to military service, it is remarkable that NS has come to be embraced by Singaporeans, as earlier noted. NS has come to be accepted as part of the Singaporean way of life because of its routinisation by the Singapore government. Initially, Singapore's conscription policy started off as a major success, as out of 9,000 called up in the first batch of national service, more than 95% reported.[37] From 1970 to 1972, the Army, Navy and Air Force increased their numbers from 10,000 to 14,000 with approximately

---

[37] Heng Chee Chan, *Singapore: The politics of survival 1965–1967*, p. 142.

8,000 reservists, from 200 to 500, and from 24 to 1,500, respectively.[38] By 1978, the size of the SAF would have increased 433% from the previous decade.[39] Even though Singapore government faced civilian resistance to national service in order to achieve its domestic 'fringe benefits',[40] the PAP government reacted to criticisms by promptly depoliticising the discussion of defence, changing the conscription policy to accommodate business interests, and illegalising public complaints of national service.[41] By the 1976 elections, conscription had ceased to be an issue of debate,[42] and remained since then as a 'social rite of passage' that all able-bodied Singapore males have had to participate in,[43] and from which "a common shared experience among the [conscripted] youth" contributed to nation-building in Singapore.[44]

Conclusion

The SAF is today widely regarded as the most modern and well-equipped armed forces in Southeast Asia, and it is tempting to

---

[38] Yuan-li Wu, "Planning security for a small nation: Lessons from Singapore", pp. 664–665.

[39] Sukhumbhand Paribatra and Chai-Anan Samudavanija, "Internal dimensions of regional security in Southeast Asia", p. 79.

[40] These benefits include the "inculcation of nationalistic values in the youth of a multiracial community and creating a pool of specialised skills," and also the inspiration of a "sense of confidence among local entrepreneurs and foreign investors" from the provision of adequate security forces in Singapore. See Obaid ul Haq, "Singapore's search for security: A selective analysis", in Stephen Chee (ed.), *Leadership and security in Southeast Asia: Institutional aspects* (Singapore: Institute of Southeast Asian Studies, 1991), p. 129.

[41] Norman Vasu and Bernard Loo, "National security and Singapore: An assessment", in Terence Chong (ed.), *Management of success: Singapore revisited* (Singapore: Institute of Southeast Asian Studies, 2010), pp. 462–485.

[42] Heng Chee Chan, *Singapore: The politics of survival 1965–1967*, pp. 143–144.

[43] Pak Shun Ng, *"Why not a volunteer army?" Re-examining the impact of military conscription on economic growth for Singapore*, Unpublished manuscript, 2003, p. 26.

[44] Elizabeth Nair, "Nation building through conscript service in Singapore", in Daniella Ashkenazy (ed.), *The military in the service of society and democracy: The challenge of the dual-role military* (Westport, CT: Greenwood Press, 1994), p. 106.

conclude that it is precisely because of its military hardware that Singapore has enjoyed relative peace and security since its independence. This is certainly an intuitive conclusion that can be drawn. However, the deterrence posture that the SAF has developed over its three generations — from the poisonous shrimp to the porcupine and, today, the dolphin is conceptually problematic.[45] We know when deterrence fails — war breaks out — but the absence of war does not necessarily mean deterrence succeeds. Nevertheless, it is also churlish at best to conclude that the SAF's deterrence posture has had absolutely nothing to do with the relative peace and security that Singapore has enjoyed throughout its history as a sovereign state.

Whether right or wrong, Singapore's policy makers have perceived a geopolitical environment in which there are multiple potential sources of threat to Singapore's existence. The policy of NS has allowed for the construction and maintenance of an SAF that has some bulk, and while it is a potentially simplistic argument, that bulk (its sheer numbers) can contribute towards the development and maintenance amongst potential adversaries that Singapore as a sovereign state can be defended, is relatively secure. This construction and maintenance of the SAF has been an expensive exercise, but without NS it could have been an even more exorbitant exercise. Finally, as has been noted earlier, the initial public unhappiness with NS has largely dissipated, and replaced by a general acceptance and embracing of the NS experience.

---

[45] Patrick Morgan argues, "It does not consistently work and we cannot manipulate it sufficiently to fix that and make it a completely reliable tool of statecraft … we do not completely know how it works." See Patrick M. Morgan, *Deterrence now* (Cambridge, England: Cambridge University Press, 2003), p. 285.

Chapter 9

Conclusion

S Vasoo and Bilveer Singh

In Chapter 1, Michael Sherraden posited the importance of asset building for societies in general and highlighted the case of Singapore in particular. Asset building is seen as the accumulation of financial and non-financial wealth that supports political and social stability. Describing Singapore as a state having one of the most advanced examples of inclusive asset-building policy, it is seen as a key strategy for social and economic development for its populace, emphasising the importance of financial as well as family and societal development, including its landmark homeownership programme. In this regard, the use of Central Provident Fund (CPF) for homeownership was seen as being particularly critical in accounting for asset building in Singapore. These were later buttressed by programmes such as Edusave, Baby Bonuses, Child Development Accounts (CDAs) and medical-related policies such as MediSave, ElderShield, MediShield Life, etc. The key to success of asset-building programmes stems from the principles of universality, progressive and lifelong, all the more as Singapore is beginning to confront the 'silver generation'.

In Chapter 2, S Vasoo tried to lay bare the rising social issues and what needs to be done in the coming years. Vasoo argued that "[i]n the next Singapore 100 (SG100), there will be some key emerging social issues which will need special attention and require new social innovative approaches for human capital development." This will require "[m]ore future social investments in terms of fund allocation, deployment of better qualified and committed social service personnel, improved facilities, enlarging volunteer base, value adding social policies and outreach service delivery can be deployed earlier to the social sectors to act as social antibodies to build the resilience of vulnerable working-class families who may slip down the ladder to achieve their human potential." The way forward would require a series of partnership but also where individuals "should be to encourage mutual help and not dependency and helplessness." As for partnerships, the model being encouraged is one where "the government, community organisations and groups, corporate sector and philanthropic individuals" are encouraged to share the social burdens.

In Chapter 3, Norshahril Saat analysed the role and importance of the approach and ideology of multiculturalism as an asset for nation building. Through hard and soft approaches, like education, socialisation and deterrent legal measures, including establishing 'out of bounds' markers, Saat argued that "multiculturalism has become part of the country's official 'narrative' and Singaporeans accept the philosophy as one strengthening the nation rather than dividing it." In view of rising ethno-nationalism and religious extremism worldwide as well as past inter-racial conflicts in Singapore, the only option for peace, security and harmony is the adoption of an accommodationist path to ensure inter-ethnic harmony. By guaranteeing minority rights and privileges, especially in racial and religious arenas, Saat argued that "Singaporeans understand multiculturalism has positive consequence for the country in the past and present," thereby embedding an asset that ensures Singapore does not crumble from within due to racial and religious conflicts. This is undertaken by guaranteeing various political, economic and social rights of all Singaporeans.

In Chapter 4, Bilveer Singh analysed the role of political innovations and stabilisers and national assets. Even though a one-party dominant state has been in existent since 1959, the political approach of widening national representation and ensuring that every racial and religious group is represented in the political system is an important approach to ensure peace and stability, and hence, a key part of asset building in Singapore. Through this approach, whatever political changes and challenges that may surface in the future, carefully thought-out political mechanisms and reforms, such as the Non-Constituency Member of Parliament (NCMP), Nominated Member of Parliament (NMP), Group Representation Constituency (GRC), Elected President (EP) and the latest, reserved EP, would ensure that the political rules of engagement act as stabilising mechanisms in Singapore. Singh argued that even though Singapore remains essentially a British Westminster parliamentary system, through creative political reforms, "a certain degree of political resilience in the system" has been embedded. These "adroit constitutional amendments and political practice" are expected "to ensure political stability, especially at a time of rising ethno-nationalism worldwide, thereby acting as powerful political stabilisers in Singapore."

In Chapter 5, Hongbo Jia and S Vasoo provided an extremely useful insight into asset building through national housing policies. Due to the very high proportion of Singaporeans being owner-occupiers of their homes, in line with Irene Y.H. Ng, Jia and Vasoo argued that housing provides financial security and assets to the populace. However, there are also other spinoffs. One of these is the role of homeownership in Singapore in enhancing the public's physiological and psychological health. Additionally, there has been the rise of increasing neighbourliness, coloration and spirit to help each other as people, who own their homes, must learn to live with each other over a long period. This led Jia and Vasoo to conclude that Singapore's housing policies have the effect of promoting social capital in Singapore, including that of bonding, bridging and linking. In multiracial Singapore, one positive outcome of the Ethnic Integration Programme has been the rise of harmonious inter-racial and inter-religious relations in the housing spaces where nearly 90% of Singaporeans live, going a long way in enhancing peace and security in the Republic.

In Chapter 6, Irene Y.H. Ng tried to show how important it was to address the needs and challenges of the lower-income in Singapore and what was being implemented that could be regarded as part of the national asset-building programme. The first thing that Ng reminded us was that the "asset holdings of low-income households are different from those of higher-income households." While the assets of the lower-income tend to be possessions that can be used to generate income and be converted to cash in times of need, over time, "these assets depreciate rather than appreciate in value." Hence, the need to understand and appreciate the challenges facing asset building of the poor compared to the middle-income or higher-income individuals. The key assets of the poor in Singapore would include their homes and personal savings, especially through CPF which also includes a medical component, even though individuals often found it difficult to service their housing loans and the situation tended to be worse for those who were in debt, be it to the public authorities or private debt providers. Ng argued that "[e]ven if low-income families have access to assets, the assets are at very basic levels" and would to be assisted, as much as possible even though individual discipline is a key to ensuring that one does not worsen one's condition through indebtedness. Still, Ng's study concluded that "asset-building policies continue to hold much promise in helping low-income families improve economically" through various governmental interventions.

In Chapter 7, Yishu Zhou and Ching Leong analysed the role of managing the nation's water resource as part of the asset-building policy. From being a water deficient and dependent state, and being regarded as one of the most "water-stressed country in the world," over the years, through various policies, Singapore has achieved a degree of self-sufficiency through the use of modern technology as well as other policies that are aimed at reducing water wastage by the public and industries. Through adroit 'water diplomacy' internationally and various measures to enhance water security, water resources are not simply seen from the perspective of human right but also a national asset that involves every citizen. While water is not free, at the same time, through socialisation, water security has been achieved, thereby strengthening national resilience of public commitment to support policies that would ensure that the tap will never be turned off.

In Chapter 8, Bernard F.W. Loo looked at the role of national conscription or national service in enhancing national security and binding the citizens towards policies that enhance nation building and bonding. Through a policy of national conscription that compelled every male citizen to be enrolled for military service and through a huge chunk of the national budget being allocated for defence, Singapore succeeded in building a credible defence capability that could safeguard the Republic's security and sovereignty. According to Loo, "conscription provided the fledgling country a platform from which to help build a national consciousness and national identity." This is an invaluable contribution from which Singapore was able to grow by leaps and bounds, despite its initial weaknesses and manifold vulnerabilities. While the role of military hardware has been vital in building the nation's defence capability, as far as its role in asset building is concerned, it is the software that is associated with national conscription that is extremely vital in explaining and understanding how national conscription can be regarded as an integral part of asset building in Singapore.

Final Remarks

Singapore's social and economic progress has not come about just based on asset accumulation and savings but more than this. It is because Singapore was fortunate that it had started off with a group of selfless leaders who were people centric and maintained social and political stability through merit and unbiased social and economic policies. Orderly leadership succession through the principle of collective leadership has ensured political stability and all-round success. With the political leaders being strategic in their outlook and through pragmatic polices of delivering the basic goods and more, the ruling party has been continuously returned to power in Singapore over the last 60 years. A stable group of visionary leaders in the government is essentially an asset to Singapore and its future survival and one cannot overlook this invaluable aspect and must not be taken for granted by majority of the populace, particularly the coming generation.

Changing demography which is population ageing is and will be an inescapable reality facing Singapore. With declining birth rate below replacement, Singapore's robustness and productivity will be seriously undermined as there will be less people to manage various institutions that drive Singapore progress. There will be less talent pool available to find effective solutions to meet the challenges of the globalising world which is undergoing both aggregative and disruptors of economy. Singapore's population has to be better equipped in terms of skills and knowledge to deal with a more interconnected world so that each and every one can find a decent living. Singapore has been able to balance the need to protert domestic interests and concerns while being open internationally to attract talented and committed people to add value to the country's population pool. In doing so, Singapore can continue to have strong asset-building capacities.

More attention has to be paid to address the issues facing working-class families and their children so that they can have better opportunities to achieve and be equipped to compete in the new and changing economy. Singapore cannot afford to sidestep the emerging income and resource gaps facing many societies as these if not tackled, can lead to future societal fractures and contention amongst various interest groups and between those have and those who do not. More steps or policy decisions can be implemented to bring about more equal opportunities through redistributive justice such as targeted approach in helping disadvantaged groups whose potential for self-help can be enhanced.

In a multiracial Singapore, there must be more transparent policies based on a compassionate merit-based principle to allocate resources for people with different ethnicity to get access to public and social services whether it be education, housing and health. Any forms of discriminations in the provision of services based on language, race or religion should not be condoned as it can cause ethnic and religious misunderstanding that can lead to societal disruptions which will not be in the interest of Singapore.

Sherraden, a keen academic observer of Singapore's progress, had discussed the importance of asset building for a state, especially a developing one. He observed that Singapore has through a multi-pronged approach, brought asset building to a higher plane as part of its state and nation building programme. The circumstances surrounding the birth of an independent Singapore in 1965 provided a powerful impetus to ensure that internal peace and unity on the one hand, and an adroit and prudent international economic, foreign and defence policy on the other, were critical factors in ensuring sound national policies. These measures ensured and enhanced national security through asset building from the very start of national governance since the early 1960s.

It was also largely responsible for the social compact between the government and governed that ensured that national programmes and policies had a very high buy-in from the public, largely explaining the strong and uninterrupted support the government has enjoyed since 1959, leading to the entrenchment of a one-party dominant state in Singapore, in turn, ensuring continuity of policies over the long run. While the concept of vulnerability has always been a powerful driver of national policies, including nation building narratives, through successful policies, Singapore has emerged as a strong state and society, and an important factor is due to the increasing assets of both the state and the people found in the political space called Singapore. With greater stability, wealth, education and inter-connectedness with the world, what was a highly goal-driven state has introduced softer policies of compassion, care and welfare, leading to the rise of a highly successful, effective, efficient, liveable, developed and secure nation.

Select Bibliography

Adamkiewicz, G., Spengler, J.D., Harley, A.E., Stoddard, A., Yang, M., Alvarez-Reeves, M., *et al.* (2014). "Environmental conditions in low-income urban housing: Clustering and associations with self-reported health", *American Journal of Public Health, 104*(9), pp. 1650–1656.

Alatas, S.H. (1977). *The myth of the lazy native.* London, England: F Cass.

Anderson, B. (2004). *Imagined communities: Reflections on the origin and spread of nationalism.* London, England: Verso.

Asher, M.G. (1995). *Compulsory savings in Singapore: An alternative to the welfare state,* NCPA Policy Report No. 198.

Attorney-General's Chambers, *Singapore statutes online, chapter VIII, offences relating to unlawful assembly.* Singapore: The Author. Retrieved on 28 December 2016 from http://statutes.agc.gov.sg/aol/search/display/view.w3p;ident=eb3d032c-5e81-4348-87ff-f88cf1e51074;page=0;query=DocId%3A%2025e7646-947b-462c-b557-60aa55dc7b42%22%20Status%3Ainforce%20Depth%3A0;rec=0

Banerjee, A.V. & Duflo, E. (2011). *Poor economics: A radical rethinking of the way to fight global poverty.* New York: Perseus Books.

Bardhan, A.D., Datta, R., Edelstein, R.H. & Kim, L.S. (2003). "A tale of two sectors: Upward mobility and the private housing market in Singapore", *Journal of Housing Economics, 12*(2), pp. 83–105.

Barr, M.D. & Low, J. (2005). "Assimilation as multiracialism: The case of Singapore's Malays", *Asian Ethnicity 6*(3), pp. 161–182.

Basu, R. (2010). "Number of homeless people doubles; more than half found sleeping in void decks; most of those picked up are placed in homes", *The Sunday Times,* 31 January 2010.

Benoit, E. (1973). *Defense and economic growth in developing countries.* Lexington, KY: Lexington Books.

Benoit, E. (1978). "Growth and defense in developing countries", *Economic Development and Cultural Change, 26*, pp. 271–280.

Beverly, S.G., Clancy, M.M. & Sherraden, M. (2016). *The early positive impacts of Child Development Accounts.* St. Louis, MO: Washington University, Center for Social Development, June.

Beverly, S.G., Sherraden, M., Cramer, R., Shanks, T.R.W., Nam, Y. & Zhan, M. (2008). "Determinants of asset holdings", in McKernan, S. & Sherraden, M. (eds.), *Asset building and low-income families* (pp. 89–152). Washington, D.C.: The Urban Institute Press.

Bin Osman, M.M. (2015). "Social issues in developing a community in Singapore", in Chan, D. (ed.), *50 years of social issues in Singapore* (pp. 189–203). Singapore: World Scientific Publishing.

Biswas, A.K. (1978). *Water development and management: Proceedings of the United Nations Water Conference, Mar Del Plata, Argentina, March 1977.* New York: Pergamon.

Bitzinger, R. (2015). "Defense industries in Asia and the technonationalist impulse", *Contemporary Security Policy, 36*(3), pp. 453–472.

Blanc, M. (1993). "Housing segregation and the poor: New trends in French social rented housing", *Housing Studies, 8*(3), pp. 207–214.

Breinig, F., Sendzik, T., Eisfeld, K. & Schmitt, M.J. (2009). "The health impacts of housing improvement: A systematic review of intervention studies from 1887 to 2007", *American Journal of Public Health, 99 Supplement 3*(S3), pp. S681–S692.

Brown, R.T., Miao, Y., Mitchell, S.L., Bharel, M., Patel, M., Ard, K.L., *et al.* (2015). "Health outcomes of obtaining housing among older homeless adults", *American Journal of Public Health, 105*(7), pp. 1482–1488.

Burgard, S.A., Seefeldt, K.S. & Zelner, S. (2012). "Housing instability and health: Findings from the Michigan recession and recovery study", *Social Science & Medicine, 75*(12), pp. 2215–2224.

Buzan, B. & Herring, E. (1998). *The arms dynamic in world politics.* Boulder, CO and London, England: Lynne Rienner.

Castells, M., Goh, B.L. & Kwok, Y.-W. (1992). "The *shek kip mei* syndrome: Economic development and public housing in Hong Kong and Singapore", *Geographical Review, 82*(2), p. 222.

Chan, A., Malhotra, C., Malhotra, R. & Østbye, T. (2011). "Living arrangements, social networks and depressive symptoms among older men and women in Singapore", *International Journal of Geriatric Psychiatry, 26*(6), pp. 630–639.

Chan, D. (ed.) (2015). *50 years of social issues in Singapore*. Singapore: World Scientific Publishing.

Chan, D., Elliott, J., Koh, G., Kong, L., Nair, S., Tan, E.S., *et al.* (2014). "Social capital and development", in Yap, M.T. & Gee, C. (eds.), *Population outcomes: Singapore 2050*. IPS Exchange Series, 1 May. Singapore: Institute of Policy Studies, Lee Kuan Yew School of Public Policy, National University of Singapore.

Chan, H.C. (1971). *Singapore: The politics of survival 1965–1967*. Singapore: Oxford University Press.

Chan, H.C. & Haq, U.H. (eds.) (1987). *The prophetic and the political: Selected speeches and writings of S. Rajaratnam*. New York: St. Martin's Press.

Chang, F. (2003). "In defense of Singapore", *Orbis*, Winter 2003.

Chang, R. (2013). "HDB to supply another 10,000 rental flats by 2017", *The Straits Times*, 17 September 2013. Retrieved from http://www.straitstimes.com/st/print/1518709

Cheong, Y.M. (1988). "The military and development in Singapore", in Djiwandono, J.S. & Cheong, M.C. (eds.), *Soldiers and stability in Southeast Asia*. Singapore: Institute of Southeast Asian Studies.

Cheung, P. (2012). "Income growth and redistribution in Singapore: Issues and challenges", in Kang, S.H. & Leong, C.H. (eds.), *Singapore perspectives 2012: Singapore inclusive: Bridging divides* (pp. 7–22). Singapore: World Scientific Publishing.

Chia, N.C. (2015). "Adding a basic pillar to the Central Provident Fund System: An actuarial analysis", *The Singapore Economic Review*, *60*(3), doi: 10.1142/S021759081550037X.

Chin, K.W. (1987). "Singapore: Threat perception and defence spending in a city-state", in Chin, K.W. (ed.), *Defence spending in Southeast Asia*. Singapore: Institute of Southeast Asian Studies.

Cho, I.S. & Križnik, B. (2017). *Community-based urban development: Evolving urban paradigms in Singapore and Seoul*. New York: Springer.

Choi, J.J., Laibson, D. & Madrian, B.C. (2004). "Plan design and 401(k) savings outcomes", *National Tax Journal*, *57*, pp. 275–298.

Chong, K.H., Yow, W.Q., Loo, D. & Patrycia, F. (2015). "Psychosocial well-being of the elderly and their perception of matured estate in Singapore", *Journal of Housing for the Elderly*, *29*(3), pp. 259–297.

Chua, B.H. (2003). "Maintaining housing values under the condition of universal home ownership", *Housing Studies*, *18*(5), pp. 765–780.

Chua, B.H. (2003). "Multiculturalism in Singapore: An instrument of social control", *Race & Class*, *44*(3), pp. 58–77.

Chua, B.H. (2014). "Navigating between limits: The future of public housing in Singapore", *Housing Studies*, *29*(4), pp. 520–533.

Chua, B.H. (2015). "Financialising public housing as an asset for retirement in Singapore", *International Journal of Housing Policy*, *15*(1), pp. 27–42.

Clarkson, P.M., Li, Y. & Richardson, G.D. (2004). "The market valuation of environmental capital expenditures by pulp and paper companies", *The Accounting Review*, *79*(2), pp. 329–353.

Coleman, J.S. (1988). "Social capital in the creation of human capital", *American Journal of Sociology*, *94*, pp. 95–120.

Colic-Peisker, V., Ong, R. & Wood, G. (2015). "Asset poverty, precarious housing and ontological security in older age: An Australian case study", *European Journal of Housing Policy*, *15*(2), pp. 167–186.

Cramer, R. & Williams Shanks, T.R. (eds.) (2014). *The assets perspective: The rise of asset building and its impact on social policy*. New York: Palgrave Macmillan.

da Cunha, D. (ed.) (2000). *Southeast Asian perspectives on security*. Singapore: Institute of Southeast Asian Studies.

Deck, R. (1999). Singapore: Comprehensive Security — Total Defence", in Booth, K. & Trood, R.D. (eds.), *Strategic cultures in the Asia-Pacific region*. New York: St. Martin's Press.

Department of Statistics Malaysia. (2016). *Current population estimates, Malaysia, 2014–2016*. Putrajaya, Malaysia: The Author. Retrieved on 9 February 2017 from http://www.dosm.gov.my/v1/index.php?r=column/cthemeByCat&cat=155&bul_id=OWlxdEVoYlJCS0hUZzJyRUcvZEYxZz09&menu_id=L0pheU4 3NWJwRWVSZklWdzQ4TlhUUT09

Department of Statistics, Ministry of Trade and Industry. (2014). *Report on the household expenditure survey 2012/2013*. Singapore: The Author.

Department of Statistics Singapore. (2015). *Yearbook of statistics*. Singapore: The Author.

Department of Statistics Singapore. (2017). *Home ownership rate of resident households*. Singapore: The Author. Retrieved on 5 July 2017 from http://www.singstat.gov. sg/statistics/visualising-data/charts/home-ownership-rate-of-resident-households

Department of Statistics Singapore. (2017). *Resident households by tenancy*. Singapore: The Author. Retrieved on 5 July 2017 from http://www.tablebuilder.singstat. gov.sg/publicfacing/createDataTable.action?refId=851

Dixon, J. (1989). *National provident funds: The enfant terrible of social security*. International Fellowship for Social and Economic Development.

Duverger, M. (1951). *Les partis politiques*. Paris, France: Armand Colin.

Dynarski, S. (2004). "Who benefits from the education saving incentives? Income, educational expectations and the value of the 529 and Coverdell", *National Tax Journal*, *57*(2), pp. 359–383.

Edelstein, R.H. & Lum, S.K. (2004). "House prices, wealth effects, and the Singapore macroeconomy", *Journal of Housing Economics*, *13*(4), pp. 342–367.

Egan, M., Katikireddi, S.V., Kearns, A., Tannahill, C., Kalacs, M. & Bond, L. (2013). "Health effects of neighborhood demolition and housing improvement: A prospective controlled study of 2 natural experiments in urban renewal", *American Journal of Public Health*, *103*(6), pp. 47–53.

Elliott, W., III & Beverly, S.G. (2011). "Staying on course: The effects of savings and assets on the college progress of young adults", *American Journal of Education*, *117*(3), pp. 343–374.

Engelhardt, G.V., Eriksen, M.D., Gale, W.G. & Mills, G.B. (2010). "What are the social benefits of homeownership?: Experimental evidence for low-income households", *Journal of Urban Economics*, *67*(3), pp. 249–258.

Falkenmark, M. (1986). "Fresh water: Time for a modified approach", *Ambio*, pp. 192–200.

Ferrari, E. (2015). "The social value of housing in straitened times: The view from England", *Housing Studies*, *30*(4), pp. 514–534.

Field, B. & Ofori, G. (1989). "Housing stress and the role of the state", *Habitat International*, *13*(3), pp. 125–138.

Finlayson, A. (2009). "Financialisation, financial literacy and asset-based welfare", *The British Journal of Politics & International Relations*, *11*(3), pp. 400–421.

Fukuyama, F. (2011). *The origins of political order*. Great Britain: Profile Books.

Gallent, N. (2014). "The social value of second homes in rural communities", *Housing Theory & Society*, *31*(2), pp. 174–191.

Ganesan, N. (1998), "Singapore in 1998: Entrenching a city-state's dominant party system", *Southeast Asian Affairs*, Singapore: Institute of Southeast Asian Studies.

Gat, A. (2005). "The democratic peace theory reframed: The impact of modernity", *World Politics*, *58*(1), pp. 73–100.

Gibson, M., Petticrew, M., Bambra, C., Sowden, A.J., Wright, K.E. & Whitehead, M. (2011). "Housing and health inequalities: A synthesis of systematic reviews of interventions aimed at different pathways linking housing and health", *Health & Place*, *17*(1), pp. 175–184.

Giddens, A. (1998), *The Third Way*. Cambridge, England: Polity.

Giliomee, H. & Simkins, C. (eds.). (1999). *The awkward embrace: One party dominance and democracy*. Cape Town, South Africa: Tafelberg.

Gittell, R.J. & Vidal, A. (2000). "Community organizing: Building social capital as a development strategy", *Contemporary Sociology*, *29*(2), pp. 352–354.

Gleick, P.H. (1993). *Water in crisis: A guide to the world's fresh water resources*. Oxford, England: Oxford University Press.

Goering, J.M. (2000). "Opening housing opportunities: Changing Federal Housing Policy in the United States", in Boal, F. (ed.), *Ethnicity and housing: Accommodating the differences*. England: Ashgate.

Grinstein-Weiss, M., Sherraden, M., Gale, W.G., Rohe, W.M., Schreiner, M. & Clinton, K. (2013). "Long-term impacts of Individual Development Accounts on homeownership among baseline renters: Follow-up evidence from a randomized experiment", *American Economic Journal: Economic Policy, 5*(1), pp. 122–145.

Ha, S.K. (2010). "Housing, social capital and community development in Seoul", *Cities, 27*(3), pp. S35–S42.

Haacke, J. (2003). *ASEAN's diplomatic and security culture: Origins, development and prospects*. New York: RoutledgeCurzon.

Habib, R.R., Mahfoud, Z., Fawaz, M., Basma, S.H. & Yeretzian, J.S. (2009). "Housing quality and ill health in a disadvantaged urban community", *Public Health, 123*(2), pp. 174–181.

Haddad, B.M. (1999). *Rivers of gold: Designing markets to allocate water in California*. Covelo, CA: Island Press.

Han, C.K. & Chia, A. (2012). "A preliminary study on parents saving in the Child Development Accounts in the Child Development Accounts in Singapore", *Children and Youth Services Review, 34*(9), pp. 1583–1589.

Haq, O.U. (1991). "Singapore's search for security: A selective analysis", in Chee, S. (ed.), *Leadership and security in Southeast Asia: Institutional aspects*. Singapore: Institute of Southeast Asian Studies.

Hardin, G. (2009). "The tragedy of the commons", *Journal of Natural Resources Policy Research, 1*(3), pp. 243–253.

Hassan, N. (2013). *Developing an analytical framework on social cohesion in Singapore: Reflections from the framing of social cohesion debates in the OECD and Europe*. Singapore: EU Centre.

He, B. & Kymlicka, W. (2005). "Introduction", in Kymlicka, W. & He, B, *Multiculturalism in Asia* (pp. 1–21). Oxford, England: Oxford University Press.

Heckman, J.J. & Masterov, D.V. (2007). *The productivity argument for investing in young youth*. Cambridge, MA: National Bureau of Economic Research.

Heo, Y.C. (2014). "The development of housing policy in Singapore and the sources of path dependence", *Housing, Theory and Society, 31*(4), pp. 429–446.

Ho, K.P. (2012). "Towards a more equal, self-reliant society", in Kang, S.H. & Leong C.-H. (eds.), *Singapore perspectives 2012: Singapore inclusive: Bridging divides* (pp. 101–107). Singapore: World Scientific Publishing.

Hodder, B.W. (1953). "Racial groupings in Singapore", *Malayan Journal of Tropical Geography*, 1, pp. 25–36.

Hoo, H.H.-W. (2016). *A study of the experience of debt, and of help received from for debt-related issues,* Honours' Thesis. Singapore: National University of Singapore.

Howard, C. (1997). *The hidden welfare state: Tax expenditures and social policy in the United States.* Princeton, NJ: Princeton University Press.

Housing and Development Board. (2013). "How is HDB helping low-income households with a roof over their head?", *Online Buzz.* Retrieved on 6 July 2017 from http://www.hdbspeaks.sg/fi10/fi10336p.nsf/cw/SuspendHigherTierRe nts?OpenDocument

Housing and Development Board. (2014). "Why can't HDB provide rental flats for all?", *Housing Speaks.* Retrieved on 6 July 2017 from http://www.hdbspeaks. sg/fi10/fi10336p.nsf/cc/PublicRentalFlats

Housing and Development Board. (2015). "2-room flexi flats". Retrieved on 5 July 2017 from http://www.hdb.gov.sg/cs/infoweb/residential/buying-a-flat/ new/2room-flexi-flats

Housing and Development Board. (2015). *HDB Annual Report 2014/15.* Singapore: The Author.

Housing and Development Board. (2015). "How can I own a BTO flat with a monthly income of $1,000?", *Housing Speaks.* Retrieved on 6 July 2017 from http://www.hdbspeaks.sg/fi10/fi10336p.nsf/cc/OwnaBTOFlatwith1000aM onth?OpenDocument

Housing and Development Board. (2015). "Lease buyback scheme". Retrieved on 5 July 2017 from http://www.hdb.gov.sg/cs/infoweb/residential/living-in-an-hdb-flat/for-our-seniors/lease-buyback-scheme

Housing and Development Board. (2016). "Fresh start housing scheme". Retrieved on 5 July 2017 from http://www.hdb.gov.sg/cs/infoweb/residential/buying-a-flat/new/schemes-and-grants/fresh-start-housing-scheme

Huang, J., Sherraden, M., Kim, Y. & Clancy, M.M. (2014). "Effects of Child Development Accounts on early social-emotional development: An experimental test", *JAMA Pediatrics, 168*(3), pp. 265–271.

Hui, W.T. (2015). "Retirement funding and adequacy", in Yahya, F.B. (ed.), *Inequality in Singapore.* Singapore: World Scientific.

Huntington, S.P. (1991). *The third wave: Democratization in the late 20th century.* Oklahoma: University of Oklahoma Press.

Hussain, Z. (2016). "Changes to political system to prepare Singapore for long term: PM Lee Hsien Loong", *The Straits Times,* 28 January 2016.

Huxley, T. (2000). *Defending the Lion City: The Armed Forces of Singapore.* St Leonards, NSW: Allen and Unwin.

Jackson, J.B. (2005). "A sense of place, a sense of time", *Design Quarterly*, *8*(164), pp. 24–27.

Jayakumar, S. & Sagar, R. (eds.) (2015). *The big ideas of Lee Kuan Yew*. Singapore: Straits Times Press.

Joo, Y.M. & Heng, Y.K. (2017). "Turning on the taps: Singapore's new branding as a global hydrohub", *International Development Planning Review*, *39*(2), pp. 209–227.

Kallidaikurichi, S. & Rao, B. (2010). "Index of drinking water adequacy for the Asian economies", *Water Policy*, *12*(S1), pp. 135–154.

Khaw, B.W. (2011, December 30). *Getting IRH to work better* [Blog message]. Retrieved from https://mndsingapore.wordpress.com/2011/12/30/getting-irh-to-work-better/

Khoo, T.C. (2009). "Singapore water: Yesterday, today and tomorrow", in Biswas, A.K., Tortajada, C. & Izquierdo, R., *Water management in 2020 and beyond* (pp. 237–250). Berlin Heidelberg: Springer.

Kim, Y., Sherraden, M., Huang, J. & Clancy, M.M. (2015). "Child Development Accounts and parental educational expectations for young children: Early evidence from a statewide social experiment", *Social Service Review*, *89*(1), pp. 99–137.

Kleevens, J.W.L. (1972). *Housing and health in a tropical city: A selective study in Singapore, 1964–1967*. Netherlands: Kominklijke Van Gorcm & Comp.

Knetsch, J.L. & Sinden, J.A. (1984). "Willingness to pay and compensation demanded: Experimental evidence of an unexpecteddisparity in measures of value," *The Quarterly Journal of Economics*, *99*(3), 507–521.

Kuah, A. & Loo, B. (2004). "Examining the defence industrialization — Economic growth relationship: The case of Singapore", IDSS Working Paper No. 70, July 2004.

Kwa, C.G. (2002). "Introduction", in Kwa, C.G. (ed.), *Beyond vulnerability? Water in Singapore–Malaysia relations*. Singapore: Institute of Defence and Strategic Studies.

Kymlicka, W. (2005). "Liberal multiculturalism: Western models, global trends, and Asian debates", in Kymlicka, W. & He, B. (eds.), *Multiculturalism in Asia* (pp. 22–55). Oxford, England: Oxford University Press.

Lang, R. & Novy, A. (2014). "Cooperative housing and social cohesion: The role of linking social capital", *European Planning Studies*, *22*(8), pp. 1744–1764.

Latif, A. (2011). *Hearts of resilience: Singapore's Community Engagement Programme*. Singapore: Institute of Southeast Asian Studies.

Lau, T.S. (1983). "National threat perceptions of Singapore", in Morrison, C. (ed.), *Threats to security in East Asia-Pacific: National and regional perspectives*. Lexington, MA: Lexington Books.

Leakey, R.E. (1977). *Origins*. New York: Rainbird.

Lee, C. (2011). "Housing affordability key to good parenting", *The Straits Times*, 25 October 2011.

Lee, E. (2008). *Singapore: The unexpected nation*. Singapore: Institute of Southeast Asian Studies.

Lee, J. (1999). *Housing, home ownership and social change in Hong Kong*. England: Ashgate.

Lee, J. (2013). "Housing policy and asset building: Exploring the role of home ownership in East Asian social policy", *China Journal of Social Work*, *6*(2), pp. 104–117.

Lee, K.Y. (1998). *The Singapore Story: Memoirs of Lee Kuan Yew*. Singapore: Singapore Press Holdings/Times Edition.

Lee, K.Y. (2000). *From Third World to First: The Singapore Story 1965–2000*. Singapore: Marshall Cavendish and Singapore Press Holdings.

Lee, N.J. & Ong, S.E. (2005). "Upward mobility, house price volatility, and housing equity", *Journal of Housing Economics*, *14*(2), pp. 127–146.

Leifer, M. (2000). *Singapore's foreign policy: Coping with vulnerability*. New York: Routledge.

Leong, C.H., Yang W.W. & Ho, H.M.W. (2014). *Singaporean attitudes to National Service*. Singapore: Institute of Policy Studies, Lee Kuan Yew School of Public Policy, National University of Singapore.

Lewis, J. & Surender, R. (2004). *Welfare state change: Towards a Third Way*. Oxford, England: Oxford University Press.

Lim, C.-Y. (1988). *Policy options for the Singapore economy*. Singapore: McGraw-Hill.

Lim, K.-L. (2001). "Implications of Singapore's CPF scheme on consumption choices and retirement incomes", *Pacific Economic Review*, *6*(3), pp. 361–382.

Lim, L.L. & Kua, E.H. (2011). "Living alone, loneliness, and psychological well-being of older persons in Singapore", *Current Gerontology and Geriatrics Research*, *2*(1), pp. 33–40.

Lim, L.L. & Ng, T.P. (2010). "Living alone, lack of a confidant and psychological well-being of elderly women in Singapore: The mediating role of loneliness", *Asia-Pacific Psychiatry*, *2*(1), pp. 33–40.

Lim, W.S.W. (1972). "Assessment of Singapore's public housing programme and its relevance to other ASEAN primate cities," *IMPACT Magazine Philippines* and *Singapore Architectural Student Magazine*, pp. 1–9.

Lister, R. (2006). "Poverty, material insecurity, and income vulnerability: The role of savings", in Sodha, S. & Lister, R. (eds.), *The saving gateway: From principles to practice*. London, England: Institute for Public Policy Research.

Loke, K.F. (2016). "F-35 fighter jet to go on display at Singapore Airshow", *Channel NewsAsia*, 9 February 2016. Retrieved on 21 March 2016 from http://www.channelnewsasia.com/news/singapore/f-35-fighter-jet-to-go-on/2501102.html

Loke, V. & Sherraden, M. (2009). "Building assets from birth: A global comparison of Child Development Account policies", *International Journal of Social Welfare, 18*(2), pp. 119–129.

Long, J. (2001). "Desecuritizing the water issue in Singapore-Malaysia relations", *Contemporary Southeast Asia, 23*(3), pp. 504–532.

Loo, B.F.W. (2012). "Goh Keng Swee and the emergence of a modern SAF: The rearing of a poisonous shrimp", in Chew, E. & Kwa, C.G. (eds.), *Goh Keng Swee: A Legacy of Public Service* (pp. 127–152). Singapore: World Scientific.

Maddocks, A., Young, R.S. & Reig, P. (2015, August 26). *Ranking the world's most water-stressed countries in 2040* [Blog message], World Resources Institute.

Madrian, B.C. & Shea, D.F. (2001). "The power of suggestion: Inertia in 401(k) participation and savings behavior", *The Quarterly Journal of Economics, 116*, pp. 1149–1187.

Madsen, W.C. (2007). *Collaborative therapy with multi-stressed families,* (second edition). New York: Guilford.

Mah, B.T. (2009, February). *Speech presented at the Committee of Supply Debate, Singapore* [Transcript]. Retrieved from http://www.mnd.gov.sg

Mani, A., Mullainathan, S., Shafir, E. & Zhao, J. (2013). "Poverty impedes cognitive function", *Science, 341*(6149), pp. 976–980.

Mannes, M., Roehlkepartain, E.C. & Benson, P.L. (2005). "Unleashing the power of community to strengthen the well-being of children, youth, and families: An asset-building approach", *Child Welfare, 84*(2), pp. 233–250.

Martin, J. (2011). "Impact of assets and the poor grows 20 years after its release", *The Source,* 13 December 2011. Retrieved from https://source.wustl.edu/2011/12/impact-of-assets-and-the-poor-grows-20-years-after-its-release/

Mathie, A. & Cunningham, G. (2003). "From clients to citizens: Asset-based community development as a strategy for community-driven development", *Development in Practice, 13*(5), pp. 474–486.

Mauzy, D.K. & Milne, R.S. (2002). *Singapore politics under the People's Action Party.* New York: Routledge.

McCarthy, D., Mitchell, O.S. & Piggott, J. (2002). "Asset rich and cash poor: Reirement provision and housing policy in Singapore", *Journal of Pension Economics & Finance, 1*(3), pp. 197–222.

McKernan, S.-M. & Sherraden, M. (eds.) (2008). *Asset building and low-income families.* Washington, D.C.: The Urban Institute Press.

Mehta, K. & Wee, A. (eds.) (2011). *Social work in the Singapore context.* Singapore: Pearson Publishing.

"MHA sets out reasons for Thaipusam restrictions", *Today Online,* 14 February 2015. Retrieved on 30 November 2016 from http://www.todayonline.com/

singapore/thaipusam-procession-poses-unique-challenges-keeping-law-and-order-mha

Middleton, A., Murie, A. & Groves, R. (2005). "Social capital and neighbourhoods that work", *Urban Studies*, 42(42), pp. 1711–1738.

Midgley, J. (1999). "Growth, redistribution, and welfare: Toward social investment", *Social Service Review*, 73(1), pp. 3–21.

"Military spending modest and purely for defence", *The Straits Times*, 6 December 1967.

Ministry of Education. (2016). *About the PSEA*. Retrieved from https://www.moe.gov.sg/education/post-secondary/post-secondary-education-account/about-the-psea

Ministry of Health. (2014). *Hospitalisation and day surgery* [Press Release]. Retrieved from https://www.moh.gov.sg/content/moh_web/home/pressRoom/Current_Issues/2014/s-3ms-resources/hospitalisation-and-day-surgery.html

Ministry of Social and Family Development. (2014). *Savings for Child Development Account*. Retrieved from https://www.msf.gov.sg/media-room/Pages/Savings-in-Child-Development-Account.aspx#

Ministry of Social and Family Development. (2014). *Statistics of children without Child Development Account (CDA)*. https://www.msf.gov.sg/media-room/Pages/Statistics-of-children-without-Child-Development-Account-(CDA).aspx

Ministry of Social and Family Development. (2016). *Approach in tackling homeless cases*. Retrieved from https://www.msf.gov.sg/media-room/Pages/Approach-in-tackling-homeless-cases.aspx

Ministry of Social and Family Development. (2016). *Community Care Endowment Fund: Annual Report for Financial Year 2015*. Retrieved from https://www.msf.gov.sg/media-room/Documents/ComCare%20Annual%20Report%20FY15.pdf

Ministry of Social and Family Development. (2016). *The Baby Bonus Scheme*. Retrieved from https://www.babybonus.msf.gov.sg/parent/

Ministry of Social and Family Development. (2017). *Baby bonus scheme frequently asked question*. Retrieved from http://www.ifaq.gov.sg/BBSS/apps/fcd_faq-main.aspx#FAQ_134031

Moravcsik, A. (1997). "Taking preferences seriously: A liberal theory of international politics", *International Organization*, 51(4), pp. 513–533.

Morgan, P.M. (2003). *Deterrence now*. Cambridge, England: Cambridge University Press.

Mutalib, H. (2002). "Constitutional-electoral reforms and politics in Singapore", *Legislative Studies Quarterly*, 27(4), pp. 659–672.

Mutalib, H. (2003). *Parties and politics: A study of opposition parties and the PAP in Singapore*. Singapore: Eastern University Press.

Mutalib, H. (2012). *Singapore Malays: Being ethnic minority and Muslim in a global city-state.* Oxfordshire, England: Routledge.

Nair, E. (1994). "Nation building through conscript service in Singapore", in Ashkenazy, D. (ed.), *The military in the service of society and democracy: The challenge of the dual-role military.* Westport, CT: Greenwood Press.

Nam, Y., Huang, J. & Sherraden, M. (2008). "Asset definitions", in McKernan, S. & Sherraden, M. (eds.), *Asset building and low-income families* (pp. 1–32). Washington, D.C.: The Urban Institute Press.

Nam, Y., Kim, Y., Clancy, M.M., Zager, R. & Sherraden, M. (2013). "Do Child Development Accounts promote account holding, saving, and asset accumulation for children's future? Evidence from a statewide randomized experiment", *Journal of Policy Analysis and Management*, 32(1), pp. 6–33.

Nathan, S.R. (2011). *An unexpected journey: Path to the presidency.* Singapore: Editions Didier Millet.

Newman, J. & Vidler, E. (2006). "Discriminating customers, responsible patients, empowered users: Consumerism and the modernisation of health care", *Journal of Social Policy*, 35(2), pp. 193–209.

Ng, I.Y.H. (2017). *One size fits all? Housing history, experiences and expectations of public rental tenants* (Social Service Research Centre, National University of Singapore).

Ng, I.Y.H. (2013). "Multi-stressed low-earning families in contemporary policy context: Lessons from Work Support recipients in Singapore", *Journal of Poverty*, 17(1), pp. 86–109.

Ng, I.Y.H. (2016). "Being poor in a rich "Nanny State": Developments in Singapore social welfare", in Lim, L.Y.C. (ed.), *Singapore's economic development, Retrospection and reflections* (pp. 279–297). Singapore: World Scientific Publishing.

Ng, I.Y.H., Lee, A., Ngiam, T.L., Ho, K.W. & Tharmalingam, N. (2012). *Longitudinal study of families placed on longer term assistance under the Work Support Programme: Second Annual Report: January to December 2011*, Unpublished report submitted to the Ministry of Community Development Youth and Sports. Singapore: National University of Singapore.

Ng, I.Y.H., Mathews, M., Ho, K.W., Ting, Y.T., Tan, J.Q. & Lim, J. (2018). *Striving for a better life: Low income families in Singapore*, Unpublished manuscript. Singapore: National University of Singapore.

Ng, I.Y.H., Ng, Y.Y. & Lee, P.C. (forthcoming). "After wage restructuring: A case study of cleaning job conditions in Singapore", *The Economic and Labour Relations Review.*

Ng, I.Y.H., Ong, Q.Y. & Theseira, W. (2017). *Debt relief: Short & medium run effects*, Unpublished manuscript. Singapore: Social Service Research Centre, National University of Singapore.

Ng, K. (2018). "Experts mixed on whether fake-news laws can protect society from 'threats of our time', *Today*, 21 March 2018.

Ng, P.S. (2003). *"Why not a volunteer army?" Re-examining the impact of military conscription on economic growth for Singapore*, Unpublished manuscript, p. 26.

Novoa, A.M., Ward, J., Malmusi, D., Díaz, F., Darnell, M., Trilla, C., *et al.* (2015). "How substandard dwellings and housing affordability problems are associated with poor health in a vulnerable population during the economic recession of the late 2000s", *International Journal for Equity in Health*, *14*(1), pp. 1–11.

O'mahony, L.F. & Overton, L. (2015). "Asset-based welfare, equity release and the meaning of the owned home", *Housing Studies*, *30*(3), pp. 1–21.

Oliver, M.L. & Shapiro, T.M. (1990). "Wealth of a nation", *American Journal of Economics and Sociology*, *49*(2), pp. 129–151.

Ong, J., Lim, M. & Seong, L. (2013). "The Singapore experience: Understanding the older persons who utilize community rehabilitation services", *International Journal of Integrated Care*, *13*(8).

Organisation for Economic Co-operation and Development (OECD). (2001). *The well-being of nations: The role of human and social capital*. Paris, France: The Author.

Organisation for Economic Co-operation and Development (OECD). (2003). *Asset building and the escape from poverty: A new welfare policy debate*. Washington, D.C.: The Author.

Paribatra, S. & Samudavanija, S.A. (1986). "Internal dimensions of regional security in Southeast Asia", in Ayoob, M. (ed.), *Regional security in the Third World: Case studies from Southeast Asia and the Middle East*. London, England: Croom Helm.

Paxton, W. (2001). "The asset-effect: An overview", in Bynner, J. & Paxton, W. (eds.), *The asset-effect* (pp. 1–16). London, England: Institute for Public Policy Research.

Paxton, W. (2003). *Equal shares? Building a progressive and coherent asset-based welfare policy*. London, England: Institute for Public Policy Research.

Pearce, D. (1995). *Blueprint 4: Capturing global environmental value*. London, England: Earthscan.

Peled, A. (1994). *Soldiers apart: A study of ethnic military manpower policies in Singapore, Israel and South Africa*. Ann Arbor, MI: University Microfilms International.

Pempel, T.J. (ed.) (1990). *Uncommon democracies*. Cornell, NY: Cornell University Press.

Phang, S.-Y. (2001). "Housing policy, wealth formation and the Singapore economy", *Housing Studies*, *16*(4), pp. 443–459.

Phang, S.-Y. (2012). *Public housing — Appreciating assets?*, Working Paper, 1397, pp. 1–7.

Piketty, T. (2014). *Capital in the twenty-first century*. Cambridge, MA: Harvard University Press.

Prabhakar, R. (2009). "The assets agenda and social policy", *Social Policy & Administration*, 43(1), pp. 54–69.

Prabhakar, R. (2009). "What is the future for asset-based welfare?", *Public Policy Research*, 16(1), pp. 51–56.

Priemus, H. (1998). "Redifferentiation of the urban housing stock in the Netherlands: A strategy to prevent spatial segregation?", *Housing Studies*, 13(3), pp. 301–310.

Public Utilities Board. (2015). *Our Water, The Flow of Progress: Annual Report 2014/2015*. Singapore: The Author.

Putman, R.D. (2000). *Bowling alone: The collapse and revival of American community*. New York: Simon & Schuster.

Putnam R.D. (2001). "Social capital: Measurement and consequences", *Canadian Journal of Policy Research*, 2, pp. 41–51.

Quah, S.R. (1998). *Family in Singapore: Sociological perspectives*. Singapore: Times Academic Press.

"Racism still a problem for some Singaporeans, CNA-IPS survey finds", *Channel NewsAsia*, 18 August 2016. Retrieved on 24 November 2016 from http://www.channelnewsasia.com/news/singapore/racism-still-a-problem/3043764.html

Rahim, L. (1996). "The paradox of ethnic-based self-help groups", in da Cunha, D. (ed.), *Debating Singapore: Reflective essays* (pp. 46–50). Singapore: Institute of Southeast Asian Studies.

Rahim, L. (1998). *The Singapore dilemma: The political and educational marginality of the Malay community*. Kuala Lumpur, Malaysia: Oxford University Press.

Regan, S. (2010). "Asset-based welfare: tackling poverty and inequality", *Public Policy Research*, 8(2), pp. 118–120.

Rohe, W.M., Key, C., Grinstein-Weiss, M., Schreiner, M. & Sherraden, M. (2017). "The impacts of individual development accounts, assets, and debt on future orientation and psychological depression", *Journal of Policy Practice*, 16(1), pp. 24–45.

Ronald, R. (2007). "Comparing homeowner societies: Can we construct an East–West model?", *Housing Studies*, 22(4), pp. 473–493.

Ronald, R. (2008). "Between investment, asset and use consumption: The meanings of homeownership in Japan", *Housing Studies*, 23(2), pp. 233–251.

Ronald, R. & Doling, J. (2010). "Shifting East Asian approaches to home ownership and the housing welfare pillar", *European Journal of Housing Policy*, 10(3), pp. 233–254.

Rose, N. (1999). *Powers of freedom: Reframing political thought*. Cambridge, England: Cambridge University Press.

Rose, N. & Miller, P. (1992). "Political power beyond the state: Problematics of government", *British Journal of Sociology*, *43*(2), pp. 173–205.

Saat, N. (2015). *Yusof Ishak: Singapore's first President*. Singapore: Institute of Southeast Asian Studies.

Saat, N. (2016). "Singapore beyond ethnicity: Rethinking the group representative constituency scheme", *The Round Table: The Commonwealth Journal of International Affairs*, *105*(2), pp. 195–203.

Salaff, J. (1990). *State and family in Singapore*. Ithaca, NY: Cornell University Press.

Sartori, G. (1976). *Parties and party systems: A framework for analysis vol. 1*. New York: Cambridge University Press.

Schreiner, M., Sherraden, M., Clancy, M., Johnson, L., Curley, J., Zhan, M., *et al.* (2005). "Assets and the poor: Evidence from Individual Development Accounts", in Sherraden, M. & Morris, L. (eds.), *Inclusion in the American Dream: Assets, poverty and public policy*. Oxford, England: Oxford University Press.

Sen, A. (1993). "Capability and well-being", in Nussbaum, M. & Sen, A. (eds.), *The quality of life* (pp. 30–53). Oxford, England: Clarendon Press.

Shanmugaratnam, T. (2015). "Inclusive housing and social equity", keynote speech at international conference sponsored by Washington University and National University of Singapore (Next Age Institute), Duke University, and Brookings Institution (host), Washington, D.C., November.

Sherraden, M. (1991). *Assets and the poor: A new American welfare policy*. New York: M.E. Sharpe.

Sherraden, M. (1992). Interview with Goh Keng Swee, National University of Singapore.

Sherraden, M. (1993). Interview with Lee Kuan Yew, Istana, Singapore.

Sherraden, M. (2003). "From social welfare state to social investment state", *Shelterforce: Journal of Affordable Housing and Community Building*, *25*(2), March/April, pp. 16–17.

Sherraden, M. (2011). "Foreword", in Mehta, K. & Wee, A., *Social work in the Singapore context*. Singapore: Pearson.

Sherraden, M. (2014). "Asset building research and policy: Pathways, progress, and potential of a social innovation", in Cramer, R. & Williams Shanks, T. R. (eds.), *The assets perspective: The rise of asset building and its impact on social policy* (pp. 263–284). New York: Palgrave Macmillan.

Sherraden, M. (2016). Discussion with Ann Wee, her residence in Singapore.

Sherraden, M. (2016). Discussion with Sudha Nair, her offices at PAVE in Singapore.

Sherraden, M., Clancy, M.M., Nam, Y., Huang, J., Kim, Y., Beverly, S.G., *et al.* (2015). "Universal accounts at birth: Building knowledge to inform policy", *Journal of the Society for Social Work and Research*, *6*, pp. 541–564.

Sherraden, M., Nair, S., Vasoo, S., Liang, N.T. & Sherraden, M.S. (1995). "Social policy based on assets: The impact of Singapore's Central Provident Fund", *Asian Journal of Political Science*, *3*(2), pp. 112–133.

Sherraden, M., Zou, L., Ku, B.H.B., Deng, S. & Wang, S. (eds.) (2014). *Asset-building policies and innovations in Asia (Vol. 3)*. London, England: Routledge.

Sherraden, M. (2009). "Individual development accounts and asset-building policy: Lessons and directions", in Blank, R.M. & Barr, M.S. (eds.), *Insufficient funds: Savings, assets, credit, and banking among low-income households* (pp. 191–217). New York: Russel Sage Foundation.

Sim, L.L., Shi, M.Y. & Sun, S.H. (2003). "Public housing and ethnic integration in Singapore", *Habitat International*, *27*(2), pp. 293–307.

Sin, C.H. (2002). "Segregation and marginalisation within public housing: The disadvantaged in Bedok New Town, Singapore", *Housing Studies*, *17*(2), pp. 267–288.

Sing, T.-F., Tsai, I.-C. & Chen, M.C. (2006). "Price dynamics in public and private housing markets in Singapore", *Journal of Housing Economics*, *15*(4), pp. 305–320.

Singh, B. (1985). "Singapore's management of its security problems", *Asia-Pacific Community*, *29*.

Singh, B. (1999). *The vulnerability of small states revisited: A study of Singapore's post-Cold War foreign policy*. Yogyakarta, Indonesia: Gajah Mada University Press.

Singh, B. (2012). *Politics and governance in Singapore: An introduction*. Singapore: McGraw Hill.

Singh, N. (2016). "Introduction", in Singh, N. (ed.), *The human right to water: From concept to reality*. New York: Springer.

Speech by Dr. Yacoob Ibrahim, Minister for the Environment and Water Resources, at the Committee of Supply Debate 2005, Part 1, 8 March 2005.

Spiess, C. (2009). *Democracy and party system in developing countries: A comparative study of India and South Africa* (Routledge Advances in South Asian Studies), 1st Edition. London, England: Routledge.

State of Singapore. (1955, February 5). Government Gazette, Extraordinary, Singapore, G.N. 309.

Stern, P.C., Dietz, T., Abel, T., Guagnano, G.A. & Kalof, L. (1999). "A value-belief-norm theory of support for social movements: The case of environmentalism", *Human Ecology Review*, *6*(2), pp. 81–97.

Steuerle, C.E., Harris, B.H., McKernan, S.-M., Quakenbush, C. & Ratcliffe, C. (2014, September). *Who benefits from asset-building tax subsidies?* (Opportunity and Ownership Initiative Fact Sheet). Washington, D.C.: Urban Institute.

Retrieved from Urban Institute website http://www.urban.org/sites/default/files/alfresco/publication-pdfs/413241-Who-Benefits-from-Asset-Building-Tax-Subsidies-.PDF

Stockholm International Peace and Research Institute (2017).

Tan, K.Y.L. & Thio, L.-A. (2015). *Singapore 50 constitutional moments that defined a nation*. Singapore: Marshall Cavendish.

Tan N.T. & Mehta, K. (eds.) (2002). *Extending frontiers: Social issues and social work in Singapore*. Singapore: Eastern Universities Press.

Tan, S.Y. (1998). *Private ownership of public housing in Singapore*. Singapore: Times Academic Press.

Teo, P.L. (2016). *Experiences of homeless families on the interim rental housing scheme in Singapore*, Unpublished doctoral dissertation. Singapore: National University of Singapore.

Thompson, S.C.G. & Barton, M.A. (1994). "Ecocentric and anthropocentric attitudes toward the environment", *Journal of Environmental Psychology, 14*(2), pp. 149–157.

Ting, W.-F. (2013). "Asset building and livelihood rebuilding in post-disaster Sichuan, China", *China Journal of Social Work, 6*(2), pp. 190–207.

Tortajada, C., Joshi, Y. & Biswas, A.K. (2013). *The Singapore water story: Sustainable development in an urban city state*. London, England: Routledge.

Toussaint, J. (2011). "Housing assets as a potential solution for financial hardship: Households' mental accounts of housing wealth in three European countries", *Housing, Theory and Society, 28*(4), pp. 320–341.

Toussaint, J. & Elsinga, M. (2009). "Exploring 'housing asset-based welfare': Can the UK be held up as an example for Europe?", *Housing Studies, 24*(5), pp. 669–692.

Tu, Y. (1999). "Public homeownership, housing finance and socioeconomic development in Singapore", *Review of Urban & Regional Development Studies, 11*(2), pp. 100–113.

Tu, Y., Kwee, L.K. & Yuen, B. (2005). "An empirical analysis of Singapore households' upgrading mobility behaviour: From public homeownership to private homeownership", *Habitat International, 29*(3), pp. 511–525.

van Gent, W.P.C. (2012). "Housing policy as a lever for change?: The politics of welfare, assets and tenure", *Housing Studies, 25*(5), pp. 735–753.

Vasil, R.K. (2000). *Governing Singapore: Democracy and national development*. Singapore: South Wind Production.

Vasoo, S. (2002). "New directions of community development in Singapore", in Tan, N.T. & Mehta, K. (eds.), *Extending frontiers: Social issues and social work in Singapore* (pp. 20–36). Singapore: Eastern University Press.

Vasoo, S. (2013). "Social work in response to challenging times", *Asia Pacific Journal of Social Work*, *23*(4), pp. 315–318.

Vasoo, S. & Lee, J. (2001). "Singapore: Social development, housing and the Central Provident Fund", *International Journal of Social Welfare*, *10*(4), pp. 276–283.

Vasu, N. & Loo, B. (2010). "National security and Singapore: An assessment", in Chong, T. (ed.), *Management of success: Singapore revisited*. Singapore: Institute of Southeast Asian Studies.

Wah, C.K. (2000). "Reflections on the shaping of strategic cultures in Southeast Asia", in da Cunha, D. (ed.), *Southeast Asian perspectives on security*. Singapore: Institute of Southeast Asian Studies.

Watson, M. (2009). "Planning for a future of asset-based welfare? New labour, financialized economic agency and the housing market", *Planning Practice & Research*, *24*(1), pp. 41–56.

Williams Shanks, T.R., Kim, Y., Loke, V. & Destin, M. (2010). "Assets and child well-being in developed countries", *Children and Youth Services Review*, *32*(11), pp. 1488–1496.

Wong, A.K. & Yeh, S.H.K. (eds.) (1985). *Housing a nation: 25 years of public housing in Singapore*. Singapore: Housing Development Board.

Wong, K. (2015). "TKMS starts construction of Singapore's Type 218SG submarines", *IHS Jane's 360*, 28 June 2015. Retrieved on 21 March 2016 from http://www.janes.com/article/52609/tkms-starts-construction-of-singapore-s-type-218sg-submarines

Wong, T. C. & Yap, A. (2003). "From universal public housing to meeting the increasing aspiration for private housing in Singapore", *Habitat International*, *27*(3), pp. 361–380.

Woolcock, M. (2001). "The place of social capital in understanding social and economic outcomes", *ISUMA Canadian Journal of Policy Research*, *2*(1), pp. 11–17.

Wu, T. & Chan, A. (2012). "Families, friends, and the neighborhood of older adults: Evidence from public housing in Singapore", *Journal of Aging Research*, *2012*(3), pp. 1–7.

Wu, Y.L. (1972). "Planning security for a small nation: Lessons from Singapore", *Pacific Community*, *3*(4).

Yap, M.T. & Gee, C. (2015). "Ageing in Singapore: Social issues and policy challenges", in Chan, D. (ed.), *50 years of social issues in Singapore* (pp. 3–30). Singapore: World Scientific Publishing.

Yeo, M. (2016). "RSAF forms 2nd local F-15SG squadron", *IHS Jane's 360*, 22 March 2016. Retrieved on 23 March 2016 from http://www.janes.com/article/58959/rsaf-forms-second-local-f-15sg-squadron

Yeo, S.J. (2015). "More public rental applicants used to be home owners", *The Straits Times*, 13 March 2015, p. A6.

Yilmazer, T., Babiarz, P. & Liu, F. (2015). "The impact of diminished housing wealth on health in the United States: Evidence from the great recession", *Social Science & Medicine, 130C*, pp. 234–241.

Index